E. S Metcalf

Olio of Isms, Ologies and Kindred Matter

Defined and Classified

E. S Metcalf

Olio of Isms, Ologies and Kindred Matter
Defined and Classified

ISBN/EAN: 9783337178895

Printed in Europe, USA, Canada, Australia, Japan

Cover: Foto ©Lupo / pixelio.de

More available books at **www.hansebooks.com**

OLIO

OF

Isms...Ologies

AND

KINDRED MATTER

DEFINED AND CLASSIFIED

Compiled by E. S. METCALF.

CHICAGO:
L'Ora Quéta P. & J. Co.
1899

THAT the reader or student may be furnished with a COMPACT and COMPREHENSIVE VIEW of questions and conclusions around which the intellectual life of man ever has and ever will revolve, this little volume of isms, ologies, and kindred matter, gleaned from the most reliable authorities, is published. It will be admitted that all ideas, whether objective or subjective, are not of equal rank and importance; that the quality, extension, and pivotal character of such are what give superiority or princely rank and value to them, and the terms that stand as their representatives. Mind is as superior to matter as life is to death. That upon which all else depends is readily admitted to be supreme; hence, subjects for consideration that involve such, pre-eminently outrank all others. We find these bearing the stately names of *isms* or *ologies*. They present themselves to us as gems, or nuggets of gold separated from their alloy. They represent the head —the heart—and the soul of the great dead past, the mighty present, the inevitable and mysterious future. While rushing on through time and space to the great unknown, catching here and there a bit of sunshine and plenty of shadow, it is believed that the reader will find it both pleasant and profitable to turn, now and then, to this volume and read, reread, and compare with easy reflection the ideas herein defined and classified, and thereby keep easily in touch with the past, and more readily understand and place value on current truths and speculations.

The matter following the isms and ologies is submitted as aids or worthy associates, and will be found generally as well as specifically useful.

E. S. METCALF.

CONTENTS.

	PAGE.
Introduction	3–10
Doctrinal and Sectarianisms	13–62
Theoretical and Scientific	63–77
Civic-isms	78–90
Miscellany	93–142
Divinations	143–149

INTRODUCTION.

ORIENTAL, GREEK, AND ROMAN PHILO-SOPHICAL SYSTEMS, B. C.

At the important era of Christ's appearance in the world, two kinds of Philosophy prevailed among civilized nations. One was the philosophy of the Greeks, adopted also by the Romans; and the other, that of the Orientals, which had a great number of votaries in Persia, Syria, Chaldea, Egypt, and even among the Jews. The former was distinguished by the simple title of *philosophy*. The latter was honored by the more pompous appellation of *science* or *knowledge;* since those who adhered to the latter sect pretended to be restorers of the knowledge of God, which was lost in the world. The followers of both these systems, in consequence of vehement disputes and dissensions about several points, subdivided themselves into a variety of sects. It is, however, to be observed, that all the sects of the Oriental philosophy deduced their various tenets from one fundamental principle, which they held in common; but the Greeks were much divided about the first principles of science.

Amongst the Grecian sects there were some who declaimed openly against religion, and denied the immortality of the soul; and others, who acknowledged a Deity, and a state of future rewards and punishments. Of the former kind were the Epicureans and Academics; of the latter, the Platonists and Stoics. The Epicureans derived their name from Epicurus, who was born in the hundred and ninth olympiad, 242 years before Christ. He accounted for the formation of the world in the following manner: A finite number of that infinite multitude of atoms, which, with infinite space, constitutes the universe, falling fortuitously into the region of the world, were, in consequence of their innate motion, collected into one rude and indigested mass. All the various parts of nature were formed by those atoms, which were best fitted to produce them. The fiery particles formed themselves into air; and from those which subsided, the earth was produced. The mind or intellect was formed of particles most subtle in their nature, and capable of the most rapid motion. The world is preserved by the same mechanical causes by which it was framed; and from the same causes it will at last be dissolved.

Epicurus admitted that there were in the universe divine natures. But he asserted that these happy and divine beings did not encumber themselves with the government of the world; yet, on account of their excellent nature, they are proper objects of reverence and worship.

The science of physics was, in the judgment of Epicurus, subordinate to that of ethics; and his whole doctrine concerning nature was professedly adapted to rescue men from the dominion of troublesome passions, and lay the foundation of a tranquil and happy life. He taught, that man is to do everything for his own sake; that he is to make his own happiness his chief end, and do all in his power to secure and preserve it. He considered pleasure as the ultimate good of mankind; but asserts that he does not mean the pleasures of the luxurious, but principally the freedom of the body from pain, and of the mind from anguish and perturbation. The virtue he prescribes is resolved ultimately into our private advantage without regard to the excellence of its own nature, or of its being commanded by the Supreme Being.

The followers of Aristotle were another famous Grecian sect. That philosopher was born in the first year of the ninety-ninth olympiad, about 384 years before the birth of Christ.

Aristotle supposed the universe to have existed from eternity. He admitted, however, the existence of a deity, whom he styled the *first mover*, and whose nature, as explained by him, is something like the principle which gives motion to a machine. It is a nature wholly separated from matter, immutable, and far superior to all other intelligent natures. The celestial sphere, which is the region of his residence, is also immutable; and residing in his first sphere, he possesses neither immensity nor omnipresence. Happy in the contemplation of himself, he is entirely regardless of human affairs. In producing motion, the deity acts not voluntarily, but necessarily; not for the sake of other beings, but for his own pleasure.

INTRODUCTION.

Nothing occurs in the writings of Aristotle which decisively determines whether he supposed the soul of man mortal or immortal.

Respecting ethics, he taught that happiness consisted in the virtuous exercise of the mind, and that virtue consisted in preserving that mean in all things which reason and prudence describe. It is the middle path between two extremes, one of which is vicious through excess, the other through defect.

The Stoics were a sect of heathen philosophers, of which Zeno, who flourished about 350 years before Christ, was the original founder. They received their denomination from a place in which Zeno delivered his lectures, which was a portico at Athens. Their distinguishing tenets were as follows: That God is underived, incorruptible, and eternal; possessed of intelligence and goodness; the efficient cause of all the qualities and forms of things; and the constant preserver and governor of the world. That matter is also underived and eternal, and by the powerful energy of the Deity impressed with motion and form. That though God and matter subsisted from eternity, the present regular frame of nature had a beginning, and will have an end. That the element of fire will at last, by an universal conflagration, reduce the world to its pristine state. That at this period all material forms are lost in one chaotic mass, all animated nature is reunited to the Deity, and matter returns to its original form. That from this chaotic state, however, it again emerges, by the energy of the efficient principle; and gods and men, and all forms of regulated nature, are renewed, to be dissolved and renewed in endless succession. That at the restoration of all things, the race of men will return to life. Some imagined that each individual would return to its former body; while others supposed that after the revolution of the great year, similar souls would be placed in similar bodies.

Those among the Stoics who maintained the existence of the soul after death, supposed it to be removed into the celestial regions of the gods, where it remains, till, at the general conflagration, all souls, both human and divine, shall be absorbed in the Deity. But many imagined, that before they were admitted among the divinities, they must purge away their inherent vices and imperfections by a temporary residence in the aerial regions between the earth and the moon, or in the moon itself. It was supposed that depraved and ignoble souls are agitated after death in the lower regions of the air till the fiery parts are separated from the grosser, and rise, by their natural levity, to the orbit of the moon, where they are still further purified and refined.

According to the doctrine of the Stoics, all things are subject to an irresistible and irreversible fatality; and there is a necessary chain of causes and effects, arising from the action of a power, which is itself a part of the machine it regulates, and which, equally with the machine, is subject to the immutable laws of necessity.

The moral doctrine of the Stoics depends upon the preceding principles. They make virtue to consist in an acquiescence in the immutable laws of necessity, by which the world is governed. The resignation they prescribe appears to be part of their scheme to raise mankind to that liberty and self-sufficiency which it is the great end of their philosophy to procure. They assert that virtue is its own proper reward, and vice its own punishment; that all eternal things are indifferent; and that a wise man may be happy in the midst of tortures. The ultimate design of their philosophy was to divest human nature of all passions and affections; and they make the highest attainments and perfection of virtue to consist in a total apathy and insensibility of human evils.

The Platonic philosophy is denominated from Plato, who was born in the eighty-seventh olympiad, 426 years before the nativity of Christ. He founded the old academy on the opinions of Heraclitus, Pythagoras, and Socrates; and by adding the information he had acquired to their discoveries, he established a sect of philosophers, who were esteemed more perfect than those who had before appeared in the world.

The outlines of Plato's philosophical system were as follows: That there is one God, an eternal, immutable, and immaterial being, perfect in wisdom and goodness, omniscient and omnipresent. That this all-wise and perfect Being formed the universe out of a mass of pre-existing matter, to which he gave form and arrangement. That there is in matter a necessary but blind and refractory force which refits the will of the Supreme Artificer, so that he cannot perfectly execute his designs; and this is the cause of the mixture of good and evil which is found in the material world. That the soul of man was derived by emanation from God; but that this emanation was not immediate, but through the intervention of the soul of the world, which was itself debased by some material admixture. That the relation which the human soul, in its original constitution, bears to matter, is the source of moral evil. That when God formed the universe He separated from the soul of the world inferior souls, equal in number to the stars, and assigned to each its proper celestial abode. That these souls were sent down to earth to be imprisoned in mortal bodies; hence proceed the depravity and misery to which human nature is liable. That the soul is immortal; and by disengaging itself from all animal passions, and rising above sensible objects to the contemplation of the world of intelligence, it may be prepared to return to its original habitation. That matter never suffered annihilation, but that the world will remain forever; but that by the action of its animating principle accomplishes certain periods, within which every thing returns to its ancient state and place. This periodical revolution of nature is called the Platonic or great year.

The Platonic system makes the perfection of morality to consist in living in conformity to the will of God, the only author of true felicity; and teaches that our highest good consists in the contemplation and knowledge of the Supreme Being, whom he emphatically styles, the *good*. The end of this knowledge is to make men resemble the Deity as much as is compatible with human nature. This likeness consists in the possession and practice of all the moral virtues.

After the death of Plato many of his disciples deviated from his doctrines. His school was then divided into the old, the middle, and the new academy. The old academy strictly adhered to his tenets. The middle academy receded from his system without entirely deserting it. The new academy, founded by Carneades, an African by birth, almost entirely relinquished the original doctrines of Plato, and verged toward the sentiments which were taught by the Skeptic philosophy.

The Skeptic, or Pyrrhonic, sect of philosophers derive their name from Pyrrho, a Grecian philosopher, who flourished at Peloponnesus, in the hundred and ninth olympiad. This denomination was in little esteem till the time of the Roman emperors; then it began to increase, and made a considerable figure.

Every advance which Pyrrho made in the study of philosophy involved him in fresh uncertainty. Hence he left the school of the dogmatists, and established a school of his own on the principle of universal skepticism.

On account of the similarity of the opinions of this sect and those of the Platonic school in the middle and new academy, many of the real followers of Pyrrho chose to screen themselves from the reproach of universal skepticism by calling themselves Academics.

Pyrrho and his followers rather endeavored to demolish every other philosophical structure than to erect one of their own. They asserted nothing, but proposed positions merely by way of enunciation, without deciding on which side, in any disputed question, the truth lay, or even presuming to assert that one proposition was more probable than another. On the subject of morals the Skeptics suspended their judgment concerning the ground of the distinction admitted by the Stoics and others, between the things in their nature good, evil, or indifferent.

The chief points of difference between the Pyrrhonists and Academics are these: The Academics laid it down as an axiom, that nothing can be known with certainty; the Pyrrhonists maintained that even this ought not to be positively asserted. The Academics admitted the real existence of good and evil; the Pyrrhonists suspended their judgment on this point. The Academics, especially the followers of Carneades, allowed different degrees of probability of opinion; but the Skeptics rejected all speculative conclusions, drawn either from the testimony of the senses or from reasoning; and concluded that we can have no good ground for affirming or denying any proposition, or embracing any one opinion rather than another.

The Eclectic philosophy was in a flourishing state at Alexandria when our Saviour was upon earth. Its founders formed the design of selecting from the doctrines of all former philosophers such opinions as seemed to approach nearest the truth, and of combining them into one system. They held Plato in the highest esteem; but they did not scruple to join with his doctrines whatever they thought conformable to reason in the tenets of other philosophers. Potamo, a Platonist, appears to have been the first projector of this plan. The Eclectic system was brought to perfection by Ammonias Saccas, who blended Christianity with the tenets of philosophy.

The moral doctrine of the Alexandrian school was as follows: The mind of man, originally a portion of the Divine Being, having fallen into a state of darkness and defilement by its union with the body, is to be gradually emancipated from the chain of matter, and rise, by contemplation, to the knowledge and vision of God. The end of philosophy, therefore, is the liberation of the soul from its corporeal imprisonment. For this purpose the Eclectic philosophy recommends abstinence, with other voluntary mortifications and religious exercises.

In the infancy of the Alexandrian school not a few of the professors of Christianity were led by the pretensions of the Eclectic sect to imagine that a coalition might, with great advantage, be formed between its system and that of Christianity. This union appeared more desirable, as several philosophers of this sect became converts to the Christian faith. The consequence was that Pagan ideas and opinions were, by degrees, mixed with pure and simple doctrines of the gospel.

The Oriental philosophy was popular in several nations at the time of Christ's appearance. Before the commencement of the Christian era it was taught in the East, where it gradually spread through the Alexandrian, Jewish, and Christian schools.

The Oriental philosophers endeavored to explain the nature and origin of all things by the principle of emanation from an eternal fountain of being. The forming of the leading doctrines of this philosophy into a regular system has been attributed to Zoroaster, an ancient Persian philosopher. He adopted the principle generally held by the ancients, that from nothing, nothing can be produced. He supposed spirit and matter, light and darkness, to be emanations from one eternal source. The active and passive principles he conceived to be perpetually at variance ; the former tending to produce good ; the latter, evil : but that, through the intervention of the Supreme Being, the contest would at last terminate in favor of the good principle. According to Zoroaster, various orders of spiritual beings, gods, or demons, have proceeded from the Deity, which are more or less perfect, as they are at a greater or less distance in the course of emanation from the eternal fountain of intelligence, among which the human soul is a particle of divine light, which will return to its source and partake of its immortality; and matter is the last or most distant emanation from the first source of being, which, on account of its distance from the fountain of light, becomes opaque and inert, and whilst it remains in that state, is the cause of evil; but, being gradually refined, it will at length return to the fountain from whence it flowed.

Those who professed to believe the Oriental philosophy were divided into three leading sects, which were subdivided into various factions. Some imagined two eternal principles, from whence all things proceeded; the one presiding over light, the other over matter, and, by their perpetual conflict, explaining the mixture of good and evil that appears in the universe. Others maintained that the being which presided over matter was not an eternal principle, but a subordinate intelligence, one of those whom the Supreme God produced by himself. They supposed that this being was moved by a sudden impulse to reduce to order the rude mass of matter which lay excluded from the mansions of the Deity, and also to create the human race. A third sect entertained the idea of a triumvirate of beings, in which the *Supreme Deity* was distinguished both from the *material* evil principle, and from the Creator of this sublunary world. That these divisions did really subsist, is evident from the history of the Christian sects which embraced this philosophy.

From blending the doctrines of the Oriental philosophy with Christianity, the Gnostic sects, which were so numerous in the first centuries, derive their origin. Other denominations arose, which aimed to unite Judaism with Christianity. Many of the Pagan philosophers, who were converted to the Christian religion, exerted all their art and ingenuity to accommodate the doctrines of the gospel to their own schemes of philosophy. In each age of the church new systems were introduced, till, in process of time, we find the Christian world divided into a prodigious variety of sentiment.*

---

*For the above introduction we are indebted to Miss Hannah Adams' "View of Religions."—ED.

PART I.

ISMS AND OLOGIES.

ISMS.

AN ISM IS A THEORY, OR DOCTRINE; ESPECIALLY, A WILD OR VISIONARY THEORY.

"The world grew light-headed, and forth came a spawn of isms which no man can number."—Goodrich.

DOCTRINAL AND SECTARIAN ISMS.

Agnosticism.

That doctrine which, professing ignorance, neither asserts nor denies. Specifically: (Theol). The doctrine that the existence of a personal Deity, an unseen world, etc., can be neither proved nor disproved, because of the necessary limits of the human mind (as sometimes charged upon Hamilton and Mansel), or because of the insufficiency of the evidence furnished by psychical and physical data, to warrant a positive conclusion (as taught by the school of Herbert Spencer);—opposed alike to dogmatic skepticism—and to dogmatic theism.

Arminian.

One who holds the tenets of Arminius, a Dutch divine, (b. 1560, d. 1609).

The Arminian doctrines are:

1. Conditional election and reprobation, in opposition to absolute predestination.

2. Universal redemption, or that the atonement was made by Christ for all mankind, though none but believers can be partakers of the benefits.

3. That man, in order to exercise true faith, must be regenerated and renewed by the operation of the Holy Spirit, which is the gift of God.

4. That man may resist divine grace.

5. That man may relapse from the state of grace.

Autotheism.

1. The doctrine of God's self-existence.
2. Deification of one's self; self-worship.

Antinomianism.

The tenets or practice of Antinomians:

ANTINOMIAN: One who maintains that under the Gospel dispensation, the moral law is of no use or obligation, but that faith alone is necessary to salvation. The sect of Antinomians originated with John Agricola, in Germany, about the year 1535.

Apostasy.

An abandonment of what one has voluntarily confessed; a total desertion or departure from one's faith, principles, or party; especially the renunciation of a religious faith; as Julian's *apostasy* from Christianity.

Asceticism.

The condition, practice, or mode of life, of ascetics.

ASCETIC: In the early church, one who devoted himself to a solitary and contemplative life, characterized by devotion, extreme self-denial, and self-mortification; a hermit; a recluse; hence, one who practices extreme rigor and self-denial in religious things.

Allotheism.

The worship of strange gods.

Anabaptism.

The doctrine of the Anabaptists.

In church history, the name Anabaptists, usually designates a sect of fanatics who greatly disturbed the peace of Germany, the Netherlands, etc., in the Reformation period.

In modern times the name has been applied to those who do not regard infant baptism as real and valid baptism.

Anglicanism.

1. Strong partiality to the principles and rites of the Church of England.

2. The principles of the Established Church of England; also, in a restricted sense, the doctrines held by the high church party.

3. Attachment to England or English institutions.

Anthropopathism.

The ascription of human feelings or passions to God, or to a polytheistic deity.

Augustinianism.

The doctrines held by Augustine or by the Augustinians.

AUGUSTINIAN: One of a class of divines, who followed St. Augustine; maintain that grace by its nature is effectual absolutely and creatively, not relatively and conditionally.

Arianism.

A denial of the Divinity of Christ.

Anathematism.

A cursing. ANATHEMA: A ban or curse pronounced with religious solemnity by ecclesiastical authority and accompanied by excommunications. Hence: Denunciation of anything as accursed.

Any person or thing anathematized, or cursed by ecclesiastical authority.

Babism.

[The title assumed by the founder, Mirza Ali Mohammed.]

The doctrine of a modern religious sect, which originated in Persia in 1843; being a mixture of Mohammedan, Christian, Jewish and Parsee elements.

Benthamism.

That phase of the doctrine of utilitarianism taught by Jeremy Bentham; the doctrine that the morality of actions is estimated and determined by their utility; also, the theory that the sensibility to pleasure and the recoil from pain are the only motives which influence human desires and actions, and that these are the sufficient explanation of ethical and jural conceptions.

Baalism.

Worship of Baal; idolatry. BAAL: The supreme male divinity of the Phœnician and Canaanitish nations.

Brahmanism.

The religion of the Brahman.

Boodh.

In Eastern Asia, a general name for Divinity.

Boodhism.

The religion of the people of Burmah.

Buddhism.

The religion based upon the doctrine originally taught by the Hindoo sage Gautama Siddartha, surname Buddha, "the awakened or enlightened," in the sixth century, B. C., and adopted as a religion by the greater part of the inhabitants of Central and Eastern Asia and the Indian Islands. Buddha's teaching is believed to have been atheistic; yet, it was characterized by elevated humanity and morality. It presents release from existence [a beatific enfranchisement, *Nirvana*] as the greatest good. Buddhists believe in transmigration of souls through all phases and forms of life. Their number was estimated in 1881 at 470,000,000.

Bitheism.

Belief in the existence of two gods; dualism.

Consubstantialism.

The doctrine of consubstantiation.

CONSUBSTANTIATION:

1. An identity or union of substance.

2. The actual, substantial presence of the body of Christ with the bread and the wine of the sacrament of the Lord's Supper; impanation; opposed to *transubstantiation*.

This view, held by Luther himself, was called *consubstantiation* by non-Lutheran writers in contradistinction to transubstantiation, the Catholic view.

Congregationalism.

1. The system of church organization which vests all ecclesiastical power in the assembled brotherhood of each local church.

2. The faith and polity of the Congregational churches, taken collectively.

In this sense (which is its usual signification) *Congregationalism* is the system of faith and practice common to a large body of evangelical Trinitarian churches, which recognize the local brotherhood of each church as independent of all dictation in ecclesiastical matters, but are united in fellowship and joint action, as in councils for mutual advice, and in consociations, conferences, missionary organizations, etc., and to whose membership the designation "Congregationalists" is generally restricted; but Unitarian and other churches are Congregational in their polity.

Clericalism.

An excessive devotion to the interests of the sacerdotal order; undue influence of the clergy; sacerdotalism.

Cenobitism.

The state of being a cenobite; a belief or practice of a cenobite.

CENOBITE: One of a religious order, dwelling in a convent, or a community, in opposition to an anchoret, or hermit, who lives in solitude.

Ceremonialism.

Adherence to external rites; fondness for ceremony.

Corporealism.

A doctrine identical with materialism.

Cosmotheism.

The doctrine that the universe is the Supreme God; a philosophical species of idolatry, leading to *Atheism*.

Chiliasm.

1. The millennium.

2. The doctrine of the personal reign of Christ on earth during the millennium.

CHILIAST : One who believes in the second coming of Christ to reign on earth a thousand years; a millenarian.

Calvinism.

The theological tenets and doctrines of John Calvin (a French theologian and reformer of the sixteenth century) and his followers, or of the so-called Calvinistic churches.

The distinguishing doctrines of this system, usually termed the *five points of Calvinism*, are, original sin or total depravity, election or predestination, particular redemption, effectual calling, and the perseverance of the saints.

It has been subject to many variations and modifications in different churches and at various times.

Druidism.

The system of religion, philosophy, and instruction, received and taught by the Druids; the rites and ceremonies of the Druids.

Druid.

A priest and poet of ancient Britons and of other Celtic nations.

Demonianism.

The state of being possessed by a demon.

Demonolatry.

The worship of demons or evil spirits.

Dogmatism.

Magisterial assertion.

Dualism.

The doctrine of two gods, a good and an evil one.

Ditheism.

The doctrine of those who maintain the existence of two gods or of two original principles (as in Manicheism), one good and one evil; dualism.

Deism.

The doctrine or creed of a deist; the belief or system of those who acknowledge the existence of one God, but deny revelation.

Deism is the belief in natural religion only, or those truths, in doctrine and practice, which man is to discover by the light of reason, independent of any revelation from God. Hence, *Deism* implies *infidelity*, or a disbelief in the divine origin of the Scriptures.

Dollardism.

The doctrines or principles of the Dollards.

Dollard.

1. One of a sect of early reformers in Germany.
2. One of the followers of Wycliff, in England.

Donatism.

The tenets of the Donatists.

Donatist.

A follower of Donatus, the leader of a body of North African schismatics and purists, who greatly disturbed the church in the fourth century. They claimed to be the true church.

Demonism.

The belief in demons or false gods.

Denominationalism.

A denominational or class spirit or policy; devotion to the interests of a sect or denomination.

Eunomian.

A follower of Eunomius, bishop of Cyzicus (fourth century, A. D.), who held that Christ was not God but a created being, having a nature different from that of the Father.

Ethnicism.

Heathenism—Paganism – Idolatry.

Euhemerism.

The theory held by Euhemerus (a philosopher, about 300 B. C.), that the gods of mythology were but deified mortals, and their deeds only the amplification in imagination of human acts.

Evangelism.

Promulgation of the Gospel.

Exorcism.

The expulsion of evil spirits from persons or places by certain adjurations and ceremonies.

Essenism.

The doctrine or the practices of the Essenes.

ESSENE: One of a sect among the Jews in the time of our Saviour, remarkable for their strictness and abstinence.

Eutychianism.

The doctrine of Eutyches and his followers.

EUTYCHIAN: A follower of Eutyches (fifth century), who held that the divine and the human in the person of Christ were so blended together as to constitute but one nature; a monophysite.

Establishmentarian.

One who regards the Church primarily as an establishment formed by the State, and overlooks its intrinsic spiritual character.

Erastianism.

The principles of the Erastians.

ERASTIAN: One of the followers of Thomas Erastus, a German physician and theologian of the sixteenth century. He held that the punishment of all offences should be referred to the civil power, and that holy communion was open to all. In the present day, an Erastian is one who would see the Church placed entirely under the control of the State.

Esotericism.

Esoteric doctrine or principles.

ESOTERIC: Designed for, and understood by, the specially initiated alone; not communicated, or not intelligible, to the general body of followers; private; interior; acroamatic; said of the private and more recondite instructions and doctrines of philosophers. Opposed to *exoteric*.

Fetichism.

1. The doctrine or practice of belief in fetiches.
2. Excessive devotion to one object or one idea; abject superstition; blind adoration.

FETICH: A material object supposed among certain African tribes to represent in such a way, or to be so connected with, a supernatural being, that the possession of it gives to the possessor power to control that being.

Formalism.

The practice or the doctrine of strict adherence to, or dependence on, external forms, especially in matters of religion.

Familism.

The tenets of the Familists.

FAMILIST: One of a fanatical Antinomian sect originating in Holland, and existing in England about 1580, called the *Family of Love*, who held that religion consists wholly in love.

Fanaticism.

Excessive enthusiasm, unreasoning zeal, or wild and extravagant notions, on any subject, especially religion; religious frenzy.

Fatalism.

The doctrine that all things are subject to fate, or that they take place by inevitable necessity.

Gallicanism.

The principles, tendencies or action of those, within the Roman Catholic Church in France, who (especially in 1682) sought to restrict the papal authority in that country and increase the power of the national church.

Genevanism.

Strict Calvinism.

Gnosticism.

The system of philosophy taught by the Gnostics.

GNOSTIC: One of the so-called philosophers in the first ages of Christianity, who claimed a true philosophical interpretation of the Christian religion. Their system combined Oriental theology and Greek philosophy with the doctrines of Christianity. They held that all natures, intelligible, intellectual and material, are derived from the Deity by successive emanations, which they call *Eons*.

Henotheism.

That form of primitive religion in which each of several divinities is regarded as independent, and is prayed to and worshiped without reference to the rest.

Hierarchism.

The principles or authority of an hierarchy.

HIERARCHY :

1. Dominion or authority in sacred things.

2. A body of officials disposed organically in ranks and orders, each subordinate to the one above it ; a body of ecclesiastical rulers.

3. A form of government administered in the church by patriarchs, metropolitans, archbishops, bishops and, in an inferior degree, by priests.

Humanitarianism.

1. The distinctive tenet of the humanitarians in denying the divinity of Christ ; also, the whole system of doctrine based upon this view of Christ.

2. (Philos.) The doctrine that man's obligations are limited to, and dependent alone upon, man and the human relations.

Hylism.

A theory which regards matter as the original principle of evil.

Hylopathism.

The doctrine that matter is sentient ; that it possesses a species of life and sensation, or that matter and life are inseparable.

Hylotheism.

The doctrine or belief that matter is God, or there is no God except matter and the universe; pantheism.

Idealism.

The system or theory that denies the existence of material bodies, and teaches that we have no rational grounds to believe in the reality of anything but ideas and their relations.

IDEAL : Intellectual ; mental ; visionary ; fanciful ; imaginary ; unreal ; impracticable ; utopian.

Immaterialism.

1. The doctrine that immaterial substances or spiritual beings exist, or are possible.

2. The doctrine that external bodies may be reduced to mind and ideas in a mind ; any doctrine opposed to materialism or phenomenalism ; especially, a system that maintains the immateriality of the soul.

Identism.

The doctrine taught by Schelling, that matter and mind, and subject and object, are identical in the Absolute ; — called also the *System or doctrine of identity.*

Infralapsarianism.

The doctrine, belief, or principles of the Infralapsarians.

INFRALAPSARIAN: One of that class of Calvinists who consider the decree of election as contemplating the apostasy as past and the elect as being at the time of election in a fallen and guilty state; opposed to *Supralapsarian*. The former considered the election of grace as a remedy for an existing evil; the latter regarded the fall as a part of God's original purpose in regard to men. (Eccl. Hist.)

Anthropomorphism.

1. The representation of the Deity, or of a polytheistic Deity, under a human form, or with human attributes and affections.

2. The ascription of human characteristics to things not human.

Jesuitism.

1. The principles and practices of the Jesuits.

2. Designing; cunning; deceitful; crafty.

JESUIT: One of a religious order founded by Ignatius Loyola, and approved in 1540 under the title of The Society of Jesus. The society was first established in the United States in 1807. The society is governed by a general, who holds office for life. The Society is an adjunct of the Roman Catholic Church, and subject to the orders of the Pope.

Jansenism.

The doctrine of Jansen regarding free-will and divine grace.

JANSENIST: A follower of Cornelius Jansen, a Roman Catholic Bishop of Ypres, in Flanders, in the seventeenth century, who taught certain doctrines denying free-will and the possibility of resisting divine grace.

Karaism.

The doctrines of the Karaites.

KARAITES: A sect of Jews who adhere closely to the letter of the Scriptures, rejecting the oral law, and allowing the Talmud no binding authority; opposed to the *Rabbinists*.

Lutheranism.

The doctrines taught by Luther or held by the Lutheran church; opposed to evils in the Catholic Church.

Latitudinarianism.

A latitudinarian system or condition; freedom of opinion in matters pertaining to religious belief.

Labadist.

A follower of *Jean de Labadie*, a religious teacher of the seventeenth century, who left the Roman Catholic Church and taught a kind of mysticism, and the obligation of community of property among Christians.

Lamaism.

A modified form of Buddhism, which prevails in Thibet, Mongolia, and some adjacent parts of Asia; so called from the name of its priests.

Magianism.

The doctrine of the Magi, who held to two principles, one good, the other evil.

MAGI: A sect of Persian philosophers. A caste of priests, philosophers and magicians, among the ancient Persians; hence, any holy men or sages of the East. An adherent of the Zoroastrian religion.

Manicheism.

A doctrine identical with that of the Magi, held by the Manichees.

Materialism.

The doctrine held by Materialists.

MATERIALIST: One who denies the existence of spiritual substances, and maintains that the soul of man is the result of a particular organization of matter in the body.

Metempsychosis.

The *pretended* passage of the soul into another body. The *pretended* passage of the soul, as an immortal essence, at the death of the animal body, it had inhabited, into another living body, whether of a brute or a human being; transmigration of souls.

Mohammedanism.

The religion or doctrine and precepts of Mohammed, the Arabian impostor, contained in the Koran; Islamism.

Monasticism.

The monastic life, system, or condition, in a house of religious retirement, or seclusion from ordinary temporal concerns.

Monothelite.

One who holds that Christ had one will only.

Monotheism.

The doctrine or belief that there is but one God.

Montanist.

A follower of Montanus, a Phrygian enthusiast of the second century, who claimed that the Holy

Spirit, the Paraclete, dwelt in him, and employed him as an instrument for purifying and guiding men in the Christian life.

Mysticism.

1. Obscurity of doctrine.

2. The Doctrine of the Mystics, who professed a pure, sublime, and wholly disinterested devotion, and maintained that they had direct intercourse with the divine Spirit, and acquired a knowledge of God and of spiritual things unattainable by the natural intellect, and such as cannot be analyzed or explained.

3. (Philos.) The doctrine that the ultimate elements or principles of knowledge or belief are gained by an act or process akin to feeling or faith.

A MYSTIC: A person who pretends to have intercourse with the spirit of God.

Millennianism.

Belief in, or expectation of, the millennium.

MILLENNIUM: A thousand years; especially, the thousand years mentioned in the twentieth chapter of Revelation, during which holiness is to be triumphant throughout the world. Some believe that during this period Christ will reign on earth in person with his saints.

Misotheism.
Hatred of God.

Modalist.
One who regards Father, Son, and Spirit as modes of being, and not as persons, thus denying personal distinction in the Trinity.

Molinism.
The doctrines of the Molinists, somewhat resembling the tenets of the Arminians.

MOLINIST: A follower of the opinions of Molina, a Spanish Jesuit (in respect to grace); an opposer of the Jansenists.

Monopsychism.
The doctrine that there is but one immortal soul or intellect with which all men are endowed.

Macedonianism.
The doctrines of Macedonius.

MACEDONIAN: One of a certain religious sect, followers of Macedonius, Bishop of Constantinople, in the fourth century, who held that the Holy Ghost was a creature, like the angels, and a servant of the Father and the Son.

Malebranchism.
The philosophical system of Malebranche, an eminent French metaphysician. The fundamental doc-

trine of his system is that the mind cannot have knowledge of anything external to itself except in its relation to God.

Manicheism.

The doctrines taught, or system of principles maintained, by the Manicheans.

MANICHEAN: A believer in the doctrines of Manes, a Persian of the third century A. D., who taught a dualism in which Light is regarded as the source of Good, and Darkness as the source of Evil.

Nativism.

Conformity with the principles or tendencies of nature; opposed to empiricism.

Naturalism.

The doctrine of those who deny a supernatural agency in the miracles and revelations recorded in the Bible, and in spiritual influences; also, any system of philosophy which refers the phenomena of nature to a blind force or forces acting necessarily or accordingly to fixed laws, excluding origination or direction by one intelligent will.

Nicene.

Pertaining to Nice, a town of Asia Minor, where the Nicene Creed was formed in A. D. 325.

Novatianism.

The doctrines or principles of the Novatians.

NOVATIAN: One of the sect of Novatius, or Novatians, who held that the *lapsed* might not be received again into communion with the Church, and that second marriages are unlawful.

Nazaritism.

The vow and practice of a Nazarite.

NAZARITE: A Jew bound by a vow to leave the hair uncut, to abstain from wine and strong drink, and to practice extraordinary purity of life and devotion, the obligation being for life or for a certain time.

Neonomianism.

The doctrines or belief of the Neonomians.

NEONOMIAN: One who advocates or adheres to new laws; especially, one who holds or believes that the Gospel is a new law.

Neoplatonism.

A pantheistic, eclectic school of philosophy, of which Plotonius was the chief (A. D. 205-270), and who sought to reconcile the Platonic and Aristotelian systems with Oriental theosophy. It tends to mysticism and theurgy, and was the last product of Greek philosophy.

Origenism.

The opinions of Origen of Alexandria, who lived in the third century; one of the most learned of the Greek Fathers.

Prominent in his teaching was the doctrine that all created beings, including Satan, will ultimately be saved.

Obscurantism.

The system or the principles of the Obscurants.

OBSCURANT: One who obscures; one who prevents enlightenment, or hinders the progress of knowledge and wisdom.

Optimism.

The opinion or doctrine that everything in nature, being the work of God, is ordered for the best, or that the ordering of things in the universe is such as to produce the highest good.

Occasionalism.

The system of occasional causes; a name given to certain theories of the Cartesian School of philosophers, as to the intervention of the *First Cause*, by which they account for the apparent reciprocal action of the soul and the body.

Occultism.

A certain Oriental system of theosophy.

OCCULT: Hidden from the eye or the understanding; invisible; secret; concealed; unknown.

Partialism.

The doctrine of the Partialists.

PARTIALIST: One who holds that the atonement was made only for a part of mankind; that is, for the elect.

Paganism.

The state of being a Pagan; Pagan characteristics; especially the worship of idols or false gods, or the system of religious opinions and worship maintained by Pagans; heathenism.

Propagandism.

The act or practice of propagating tenets, carrying from place to place, as the Christian religion.

Premonstratensian.

One of a religious order of regular canons founded by St. Norbert at Premontre, in France, in 1119. The members of the order are called also *White Canons*, *Norbertines*, and *Premonstrants*.

Presbyterianism.

That form of church government which invests presbyters with all spiritual power and admits no prelates over them; also, the faith and quality of the Presbyterian church, taken collectively.

Plymouth Brethren.

The members of a religious sect which first appeared at Plymouth, England, about 1830. They protest against Sectarianism, and reject all official ministry or clergy.

Polytheism.

The doctrine of, or belief in, a plurality of gods.

Positivism.

A system of philosophy originated by M. Auguste Conte, which deals only with *positives*. It excludes from philosophy everything but the natural phenomena or properties of knowable things, together with their invariable relations of co-existence and succession, as occurring in time and space. Such relations are denominated laws, which are to be discovered by observation, experiment, and comparison. This philosophy holds all inquiry into causes, both efficient and final, to be useless and unprofitable.

Prelatism.

Pertaining to prelates or prelacy.

Patriarchism.

Government by patriarch, or the head of the family.

Patripassian.

One of a body of believers in the early church who denied the independent pre-existent personality of Christ, and who, accordingly, held that the Father suffered with the Son.

Paulician.

One of a sect of Christian dualists originating in Armenia in the seventh century. They rejected the Old Testament and a part of the New one.

Perfectionism.

The doctrine of the Perfectionists.

PERFECTIONIST: One pretending to perfection; especially, one pretending to moral perfection; one who believes that persons may and do attain moral perfection and stainlessness in this life.

Pantheism.

The doctrine that the universe taken or conceived of as a whole is God; the doctrine that there is no

God, but the combined forces and laws which are manifested in the existing universe; cosmotheism.

Platonism.

1. The doctrines or philosophy of Plato or of his followers.

2. An elevated, rational, and ethical conception of the laws and forces of the universe; sometimes imaginative or fantastic philosophical notions. Plato held to two eternal causes, God and matter.

Plotinist.

A disciple of Plotinus, a celebrated Platonic philosopher of the third century, who taught that the human soul emanates from the divine Being, to whom it is reunited at death.

Phalansterism.

A system of Phalansteries proposed by Fourier; Fourierism.

PHALANSTERY: An association or community organized under the plan of Fourier.

Pharisaism.

1. The notions, doctrines, and conduct of the Pharisees, as a sect. Rigid observance of external forms of religion without genuine piety; hypocrisy in re-

ligion ; a censorious, self-righteous spirit in matters of morals or manners.

PHARISEE : One of a sect or party among the Jews noted for a strict and formal observance of rights and ceremonies and of the traditions of the elders, and whose pretensions to superior sanctity led them to separate themselves from the other Jews.

Pietism.

The principles or practice of the Pietists.

PIETIST : One of a class of religious reformers in Germany in the seventeenth century, who sought to revive declining piety in the Protestant churches ; often applied as a term of reproach to those who make a display of religious feeling.

Psychism.

The doctrine of Quesne, that there is a fluid universally diffused, and equally animating all living beings, the difference in their actions being due to the difference of the individual organizations.

Pillarist.

One of an ancient sect of Christians who stood continually on a pillar.

Patripassians.

A sect of religionists who held that God, the Father, suffered with Christ.

Pedobaptism.

The doctrine of those who hold to infant baptism.

Psychopannychism.

The doctrine that the soul falls asleep at death and does not wake until the resurrection of the body.

Purgatory.

A state or place of purification after death ; according to the Roman Catholic creed, a place or a state believed to exist after death, in which the souls of persons are purified by expiating such offenses committed in this life as do not merit eternal damnation, or in which they fully satisfy the justice of God for sins that have been forgiven. After this purgation from the impurities of sin, the souls are believed to be received into heaven.

PURGATORIAN : One who holds to the doctrine of Purgatory.

Puritanism.

The doctrines, notions, or practice of Puritans.

Puseyism.

The principles of Dr. Pusey and others at Oxford, England, as exhibited in various publications, especially in a series which appeared from 1833 to 1841, designated "Tracts for the Times"; tractarianism.

Protestantism.

The quality or state of being protestant, especially against the Roman Catholic Church; the principles or religion of the Protestants.

Psilanthropism.

The doctrine that Christ was a mere man.

Predestinarianism.

The system or doctrine of the Predestinarians. The purpose of God from eternity respecting all events; especially, the preordination of men to everlasting happiness or misery.

Prelatist.

One who supports or advocates prelacy, or the government of the church by prelates; hence, a high-churchman.

Pyrrhonism.

From Pyrrho, the founder of a school of skeptics in Greece (about 300 B. C.) Skepticism; universal doubt.

PYRRHONIST: A follower of Pyrrho, a skeptic.

Pythagorism.

The doctrine of Pythagoras or the Pythagoreans. Pythagoras made numbers the basis of his philosophical system, as well physical as metaphysical. The doctrine of the transmigration of souls (Metempsychosis) is associated closely with the name of Phythagoras.

Quietism.

The system of the Quietists, who maintained that religion consists in the withdrawal of the mind from worldly interests and anxieties, and its constant employment in the passive contemplation of God and his attributes.

QUIETIST: One of a sect of Mystics originated in the seventeenth century by Molinos, a Spanish priest, living in Rome.

Rationalism.

1. The doctrine or system of those who deduce their religious opinions from reason or the understanding, as distinct from, or opposed to, revelation.

2. The system that makes *rational* power the ultimate test of truth; opposed to sensualism, or sensationalism and empiricism.

Romanism.

The tenets of the church of Rome; the Roman Catholic religion.

Recusant.

One who refuses to conform to the rights of the Established Church of England. Refusing to acknowledge the supremacy of the king.

Sabbatism.

Rest, intermission of labor.

SABBATARIAN : One who regards and keeps the seventh day of the week holy, agreeably to the letter of the Fourth Commandment in the Decalogue.

Satanism.

A diabolical spirit ; the evil and malicious dispositions of Satan.

SATAN : The great adversary ; the devil ; the chief of the fallen angels.

Sabianism.

Worship of the Sun, Moon and Stars

Shintoism.

One of the two great systems of religious belief in Japan. Its essence is ancestor worship, and sacrifice to dead heroes.

Scholasticism.

The methods or subtleties of the schools of philosophy ; scholastic formality ; scholastic doctrines or philosophy.

Shamanism.

The type of religion which once prevailed among all the Ural-Altaic peoples (Hungusic, Mongol and Turkish), and which still survives in various parts of Northern Asia. The Shaman, or wizard priest, deals with good as well as evil spirits, especially the good spirits of ancestors.

Sectarianism.

The quality or character of a Sectarian; devotion to the interests of the party; excess of partisan or devotional zeal; adherence to a separate church organization.

SECTARIAN: One of a sect; a member or adherent of a special school, denomination, or religious or philosophical party; one of a party in religion which has separated itself from an established church, or which holds tenets different from those of the prevailing denomination in a state.

SECT: Those following a particular leader or authority, or attached to a certain opinion; a company or set having a common belief or allegiance distinct from others; in religion, the believers in a particular creed, or upholders of a particular practice; especially, in modern times, a party dissenting from an established church ; a denomination ; in philosophy, the disciples of a particular master ; a school ; in society and the state, an order, rank, class, or party.

Supralapsarians.

The Supralapsarians are persons who hold that God, without any regard to the good or evil works of men, has resolved, by an eternal decree, *supra lapsum*, antecedently to any knowledge of the fall of Adam, and independently of it, to save some and reject others ; or in other words, that God intended to glorify his justice in the condemnation of some, as well as his mercy in the salvation of others ; and for that purpose, decreed that Adam should necessarily fall.

Stoicism.

1. The opinions and maxims of the Stoics.
2. A real or pretended indifference to pleasure or pain ; insensibility ; impassiveness.

STOIC: A disciple of the philosopher Zeno ; one of a Greek sect which held that men should be free from passion, unmoved by joy, or grief, and should submit without complaint to unavoidable necessity, by which things are governed.

Sufism.

A refined mysticism among certain classes of Mohammedans, particularly in Persia, who hold to a kind of pantheism, and practice extreme asceticism in their lives.

Swedenborgianism.

The doctrine of the Swedenborgians.

SWEDENBORGIAN: One who holds the doctrine of the New Jerusalem church, as taught by Emanuel Swedenborg, a Swedish philosopher and religious writer, who was born A. D. 1688 and died 1772. Swedenborg claimed to have direct intercourse with the spiritual world through the opening of his spiritual senses in 1745. He taught that the Lord Jesus Christ, as comprehending in himself all the fullness of the Godhead, is the one only God; and that there is a spiritual sense to the Scriptures which he (Swedenborg) was able to reveal, because he saw the correspondence between natural and spiritual things.

Supernaturalism.

1. The quality or state of being supernatural.

2. (Theology.) The doctrine of a divine and supernatural agency in the production of the miracles and revelations recorded in the Bible, and in the

grace which renews and sanctifies men ; in opposition to the doctrine which denies the agency of another than physical or natural causes in the case.

Syncretism.

Attempted union of principles or parties irreconcilably at variance with each other.

SYNCRETIST: One who attempts to unite principles or parties which are irreconcilably at variance; especially an adherent of George Calixtus and other Germans of the seventeenth century, who sought to unite or reconcile the Protestant sects with each other and with the Roman Catholics, and thus occasioned a long and violent controversy in the Lutheran Church.

Spinozism.

The doctrines of Spinoza, consisting in Atheism and Pantheism.

Spiritualism.

The doctrine that all that exists is spirit or soul as distinct from materialism; the doctrine of the existence of spirits as distinct from matter; the state of being spiritual.

Sabbatarianism.

Of, or pertaining to, the Sabbath, or the tenets of the Sabbatarians.

SABBATARIAN: One who regards and keeps the seventh day of the week as holy, agreeably to the letter of the Fourth Commandment in the Decalogue.

There were Christians in the early church who held this opinion, and certain Christians, especially the Seventh Day Baptists, hold it now.

Sabellianism.

The doctrines or tenets of Sabellius.

SABELLIAN: A follower of the Sabellius, a presbyter of Ptolemais in the third century, who maintained that there is but one person in the Godhead, and that the Son and Holy Spirit are only different powers, operations, and offices of the one God the Father.

Sabianism.

The doctrine of the Sabians; the Sabian religion; that species of idolatry which consists in worshiping the sun, moon, and stars; heliolatry.

Sentiment.

A thought prompted by passion or feeling; a state of mind in view of some subject; feeling toward or respecting some person or thing; disposition prompting to action or expression.

Syn.—Thought; opinion; notion; sensibility; feeling; sentiment.

OPINION, FEELING. An *opinion* is an intellectual judgment in respect to any and every kind of truth. *Feeling* describes those affections of pleasure and pain which spring from the exercise of our sentient and emotional powers. SENTIMENT (particularly in the plural) lies between them, denoting *settled opinions* or principles in regard to subjects which interest the feelings strongly, and are presented more or less constantly in practical life. Hence, it is more appropriate to speak of our religious *sentiments* than *opinions*, unless we mean to exclude all reference to our feelings. The word *sentiment* in the singular, leans ordinarily more to the side of feeling, and denotes a refined sensibility on subjects affecting the heart. "On questions of feeling, taste, observation, or report we define our *sentiments*. On questions of science, argument, or metaphysical abstraction we define our *opinions*. The *sentiments* of the heart. The *opinions* of the mind. There is more of instinct in *sentiment*, and more of definition in *opinion*. The admiration of a work of art which results from first impressions, is classed with our *sentiments;* and, when we have accounted to ourselves for the approbation, it is classed with our *opinions*."—*W. Taylor.*

Sentimental.

Having, expressing, or containing a sentiment or sentiments; abounding with moral reflections; containing a moral reflection; didactic.

Syn.—ROMANTIC, SENTIMENTAL. SENTIMENTAL usually describes an error or excess of the *sensibilities;* ROMANTIC, a vice of the imagination. The votary of the former gives indulgence to his *sensibilities* for the mere luxury of their excitement; the votary of the latter allows his imagination to rove for the pleasure of creating scenes of *ideal* enjoyment. "Perhaps there is no less danger in works called *sentimental.* They attack the heart more successfully because more cautiously."—*V. Knox.*

"I can not but look on an indifference of mind as to the good or evil things of this life as a mere *romantic* fancy of such who would be thought to be much wiser than they ever were or could be."—*Stillingfleet.*

Sacramentalism.

The doctrine and use of sacraments; attachment of excessive importance to sacraments.

SACRAMENTALIST: One who holds the doctrine of the real objective presence of Christ's body and blood in the Holy Eucharist.

Sacramentarian.

A name given in the sixteenth century to those German reformers who rejected both the Roman and Lutheran doctrine of the Holy Eucharist.

Socinianism.

The tenets or doctrines of Faustus Socinus, an Italian theologian of the sixteenth century, who denied the Trinity, the deity of Christ, the personality of the devil, the native and total depravity of man, the vicarious atonement, and the eternity of future punishment.

His theory was, that Christ was a man divinely commissioned, who had no existence before he was conceived by the Virgin Mary; that human sin was the imitation of Adam's sin, and that human salvation was the imitation and doctrine of Christ's virtue; that the Bible was to be interpreted by human reason; and that its language was metaphorical, and not to be taken literally.

Skepticism.

1. An undecided, inquiring state of mind; doubt, uncertainty.

2. The doctrine that no fact or principle can be certainly known; the tenet that all knowledge is

uncertain, Pyrrhonism; universal doubt; the position that no fact or truth, however worthy of confidence, can be established on philosophical grounds; critical investigation or inquiry, as opposed to the positive assumption or assertion of certain principles.

3. A doubting of the truth of revelation, or a denial of the divine origin of the Christian religion, or of the being, perfection, or truth of God.

Sentimentalism.

The quality of being sentimental; the character or behavior of a sentimentalist; sentimentality.

Schwenkfeldian.

A religious sect founded by Kasper von *Schwenkfeld*, a Silesian reformer, who disagreed with Luther, especially on the deification of the body of Christ.

Transcendentalism.

(Kantian Philosophy.) The transcending or going beyond, empiricism, and ascertaining *a priori;* the fundamental principles of human knowledge.

Transcendental.

1. Supereminent; surpassing others; as Transcendental being or qualities.

2. (Philos.) In the Kantian system, of or pertaining to that which can be determined *a priori* in regard to the fundamental principles of all human knowledge, or become *transcendent*. It simply signifies *a priori* or necessary conditions of experience which, though affording the condition of experience, *transcend* the sphere of that contingent knowledge which is acquired by experience.

3. Vaguely and ambitiously extravagant in speculation, imagery, or diction.

Syn.—TRANSCENDENTAL, EMPIRICAL. These terms, with the corresponding nouns, *transcendentalism* and *empirism*, are of comparatively recent origin. *Empirical*, refers to knowledge which is gained by the experience of actual phenomena, without reference to the principles or laws to which they are to be referred, or by which they are to be explained. *Transcendental* has reference to those beliefs or principles which are not derived from experience, and yet are absolutely necessary to make experience possible or useful. Such in the better sense of the term, is the *transcendental* philosophy, or *Transcendentalism*. Each of these words is also used in a bad sense, *Empiricism* applying to that one-sided view of knowledge which neglects or loses sight of the truths or principles referred to above, and trusts to experience alone; *Transcendentalism* to the opposite extreme, which, in its deprecation of experience loses sight of the relations, which facts and phenomena sustain to principles, and hence to a kind of philosophy, or a use of language, which is vague, obscure, fantastic, or extravagant.

Tavism.

One of the popular religions of China, sanctioned by the state.

Theocrasy.

1. A mixture of the worship of different gods, as of Jehovah and of idols.
2. (Philos.) An intimate union of the soul with God in contemplation, an ideal of the Neoplatonists and of some Oriental mystics.

Theodicy.

A vindication of the justice of God in ordaining or permitting natural and moral evil

Tritheism.

A belief in three Gods.

TRITHEIST: One who believes that there are three Gods in the Godhead.

Theosophy.

Much is said nowadays about theosophy, which is really but another name for mysticism. It is not a philosophy, for it will have nothing to do with philosophical methods; it might be called a religion, though it has never had a following large enough to make a very strong impression on the world's religious history. The name is from the Greek word *theosophia*—divine wisdom—and the object of theosophical study is professedly to understand the nature of divine things. It differs, however, from both philosophy and theology, even when these have the same object of investigation. For, in seeking to learn the divine nature and attributes, philosophy employs the methods and principles of natural reasoning; theology uses these, adding to them certain principles derived from revelation. Theosophy, on the other hand, professes to exclude all reasoning processes as imperfect, and to derive its knowledge from direct communication with God himself. It does not, therefore, accept the truths of recorded revelation as immutable, but as subject to modification by later direct and personal revelations. The theosophical idea has had followers from the earliest times. Since the Christian era we may class among theosophists such sects as Neoplatonists, the Hesychasts of the Greek Church, the Mystics of mediæval times, and, in later times, the disciples of Paracelus, Thalhuser, Bohme, Swedenborg, and others. Recently a small sect has arisen which has taken the name of Theosophists. Its leader was an English gentleman who had become fascinated with the doctrine of Buddhism. Taking a few of his followers to India, they have been prosecuting their studies there, certain individuals attracting considerable attention by claim of miraculous powers. It need hardly be said that the revelations they have claimed to receive have been, thus far, without element of benefit to the human race.

THEOSOPHIST: The *theosophist* is one who gives a theory of God, or of the works of God, which has not reason, but an inspiration of his own, for its basis.—*R. A. Vaughan.*

Theogonism.

The generation or genealogy of the gods; that branch of heathen theology which deals with the origin and descent of the deities.

Tritheism.

A belief in three Gods, in the Godhead.

Theism.

Belief in the existence of God.

Theosophism.

Pretension to divine illumination; enthusiasm.

Ultramontanism.

The principles of those within the Roman Catholic Church who maintain extreme views favoring the Pope's supremacy; so used by those living north of the Alps in reference to the Italians; rarely used in an opposite sense, as referring to the views of those living north of the Alps and opposed to the papal claims.

ULTRAMONTANE :

1. One who resides beyond the mountains, especially beyond the Alps; a foreigner.
2. One who maintains extreme views favoring the Pope's supremacy.

Unitarianism.

The doctrine of Unitarians, which denies the Trinity idea, and ascribes divinity to God the Father only.

Universalism.

The belief that all men will be saved, or made happy in a future life.

Utilitarianism.

1. The doctrine that the greatest happiness of the greatest number should be the end and aim of all social and political institutions.—*Bentham.*

2. The doctrine that virtue is founded in utility, or that virtue is defined and enforced by its tendency to promote the highest happiness of the universe.—*J. S. Mill.*

3. The doctrine that utility is the sole standard of morality, so that the rectitude of an action is determined by its usefulness.

UTILITARIAN: One who holds the doctrine of utilitarianism. The Utilitarians are for merging all the particular virtues into one, and would substitute in their place the greatest usefulness, as the alone principle to which every question respecting the morality of actions should be referred.—*Chalmers.*

CIVIC ISMS.

Anarchism.

The doctrine or practice of Anarchists.

ANARCHY : Absence of government; the state of society where there is no law or supreme power ; a state of lawlessness ; political confusion.

Anticivism.

Opposition to the body politic of citizens.

Boycottism.

Methods of boycotters.

BOYCOTT : A process, fact, or pressure of boycotting; a combining to withhold or prevent dealings or social intercourse with a tradesman, employer, etc.; social and business interdiction for the purpose of coercion. [Boycott, — from Captain Boycott, a land agent in Mayo, Ireland, so treated in 1880.]

Bureaucracy.

1. A system of carrying on the business of government by means of departments or bureaus, each under the control of a chief, in contradistinction to a system in which the officers of government

have an associated authority and responsibility; also, government conducted on this system.

2. Government officials, collectively.

Bimetallism.

The legalized use of two metals (as gold and silver) in the currency of a country, at a fixed relative value; in opposition to *monometallism*.

Collectivism.

The doctrine that land and capital should be owned by society collectively or as a whole; communism.

Chartism.

In England the discontent of the laboring classes of the people at the distinction in society.

Civism.

Patriotism, love or care of the public.

Caesarism.

A system of government in which unrestricted power is exercised by a single person, to whom, as Cæsar or emperor, it has been committed by the popular will; imperialism; also, advocacy or support of such a system of government. This word came into prominence in the time of Napoleon III., as an expression of the claims and political views of that emperor, and of the politicians of his court.

Cyphonism.

A punishment sometimes used by the ancients, consisting in the besmearing of the criminal with honey, and exposing him to insects. It is still in use among some Oriental nations.

Communalism.

A French theory of government which holds that each commune should be a kind of independent state, and the national government a confederation of such states having only limited powers.

It is advocated by advanced French republicans; but it should not be confounded with communism.

Communism.

A scheme of equalizing the social conditions of life; specifically, a scheme which contemplates the abolition of inequalities in the possession of property, as by distributing all wealth equally to all, or by holding all wealth in common for the equal use and advantage of all.

Carbonarism.

The principles, practices, or organization of the **Carbonari**.

have an associated authority and responsibility; also, government conducted on this system.

2. Government officials, collectively.

Bimetallism.

The legalized use of two metals (as gold and silver) in the currency of a country, at a fixed relative value; in opposition to *monometallism*.

Collectivism.

The doctrine that land and capital should be owned by society collectively or as a whole; communism.

Chartism.

In England the discontent of the laboring classes of the people at the distinction in society.

Civism.

Patriotism, love or care of the public.

Caesarism.

A system of government in which unrestricted power is exercised by a single person, to whom, as Cæsar or emperor, it has been committed by the popular will; imperialism; also, advocacy or support of such a system of government. This word came into prominence in the time of Napoleon III., as an expression of the claims and political views of that emperor, and of the politicians of his court.

Cyphonism.

A punishment sometimes used by the ancients, consisting in the besmearing of the criminal with honey, and exposing him to insects. It is still in use among some Oriental nations.

Communalism.

A French theory of government which holds that each commune should be a kind of independent state, and the national government a confederation of such states having only limited powers.

It is advocated by advanced French republicans; but it should not be confounded with communism.

Communism.

A scheme of equalizing the social conditions of life; specifically, a scheme which contemplates the abolition of inequalities in the possession of property, as by distributing all wealth equally to all, or by holding all wealth in common for the equal use and advantage of all.

Carbonarism.

The principles, practices, or organization of the Carbonari.

tained by the people, but is indirectly exercised through a system of representation and delegated authority periodically renewed; a constitutional representative government; a republic.

Despotism.

Absolute power.

Demagogism.

The practices of demagogues; leaders of the populace by questionable methods.

Exclusionism.

The character, manner or principles of an Exclusionist.

EXCLUSIONIST: One who would exclude another from some right or privilege; especially, one of the anti-popish politicians of the time of Charles II.

Fenianism.

The principles, purposes and methods, of the Fenians.

FENIAN: A member of a secret organization, consisting mainly of Irishmen, having for its aim the overthrow of English rule in Ireland.

Feudalism.

The feudal system; a system by which the holding of estates is made dependent upon an obligation to render military service to the king or feudal superior ; feudal principles and usages.

Filibusterism.

The characteristics or practices of a Filibuster.

FILIBUSTER : A lawless military adventurer, especially one in quest of plunder ; a freebooter ; originally applied to buccaneers infesting the Spanish-American coasts, but introduced into common English to designate the followers of Lopez in his expedition to Cuba in 1851, and those of Walker in his expedition to Nicaragua in 1855.

Incivism.

Want of civism or patriotism.

Individualism.

The state of individual interest or attachment to the interest of an individual in preference to the common interests of society.

Jacobinism.

Unreasonable opposition to government.

JACOBIN :

1. A Dominican Friar ;—so named because, before the French Revolution, that order had a convent in the Rue St. Jacques, Paris.

2. One of a Society of violent agitators in France, during the Revolution, 1789, who held secret meetings to control the proceedings of the National Assembly. Hence: A plotter against an existing government; a turbulent demagogue; a partisan of James II. of England.

Know-nothingism.

The doctrines, principles, or, practices, of the Know-nothings.

KNOW-NOTHING: A member of a secret political organization in the United States, the chief objects of which were the proscription of foreigners by the repeal of the naturalization laws, and the exclusive choice of native Americans for office.

The party originated in 1853, and existed for about three years. The members of it were called Know-nothings, because they replied, "I don't know," to any question asked them in reference to the party.

Legitimism.

The principles or plans of Legitimists.

LEGITIMIST:

1. One who supports legitimate authority; especially one who believes in hereditary monarchy as a divine right.

2. Specifically, a supporter of the claims of the elder branch of the Bourbon dynasty to the crown of France.

Liberalism.

Liberal principles; the principles and methods of the Liberals in politics or religion; specifically the principles of the Liberal party.

Machiavelianism.

The supposed principles of Machiavel; or practice in conformity to them; political artifice, intended to favor arbitrary power.

Militarism.

A military state or condition; reliance on military force in administering government.

Malthusianism.

The system of Malthusian doctrines relating to population.

Nepotism.

Undue attachment to relations; favoritism shown to members of one's family; bestowal of patronage in consideration of relationship, rather than of merit or of legal claim.

Nihilism.

1. The doctrine that nothing can be known; skepticism as to all knowledge and all reality.

2. The theories and practices of the Nihilists.

NIHILIST:

1. One who advocates the doctrines of Nihilism; one who believes or teaches that nothing can be known, or asserted to exist.

2. A member of a secret association (especially in Russia), which is devoted to the destruction of the present political, religious, and social institutions.

Nationalism.

1. The state of being national; national attachment; nationality.

2. An idiom, trait or character peculiar to any nation.

3. National independence; the principles of the Nationalists.

NATIONALIST: One who advocates national unity and independence: one of the party favoring Irish independence.

Oligarchy.

A form of government in which the supreme power is placed in the hands of a few persons, also, those who form the ruling few

Optimacy.

Government by the nobility.

OPTIMATE: A noble man or aristocrat; a chief

man in a state or city. The nobility or aristocracy of ancient Rome, as opposed to the *Populares*.

Patriotism.

"Love of one's country; devotion to the welfare of one's country; the virtues and actions of a patriot; the passion which inspires one to serve his country."
—*Berkeley*.

Phalansterianism.

The system of social organization recommended by Charles Fourier.

Pan-hellenism.

A scheme to unite all of the Greeks in one political body.

Pan-islamism.

A desire or plan for the union of all Mohammedan nations for the conquest of the world.

Pan-slavism.

A scheme or desire to unite all the Slavic nations into one confederacy.

Paternalism.

The theory or practice of paternal government; the assumption by the governing power of a quasi-fatherly relation to the people, involving strict and intimate supervision of their business and social concerns, upon the theory that they are incapable of managing their own affairs.

Protectionism.

The doctrine or policy of Protectionists. (Polit. Econ.) A theory or policy of protecting the producers in a country from foreign competition in the home market by the imposition of such discriminating duties on goods of foreign production as will restrict or prevent their importation;—opposed to *free trade*.

Radicalism.

The doctrine or principles of making reform in government.

RADICAL : (Politics) One who advocates radical changes in government or social institutions, especially such changes as are intended to level class inequalities;—opposed to *conservative*.

Royalism.

Attachment to a kingly government.

Republicanism.

System of Republican government.

1. A republican form or system of government; the principles or theory of republican government. Republican Party. (United States Politics.) An

earlier name of the Democratic party when it was opposed to the Federal party. Thomas Jefferson was its great leader.

2. One of the existing great parties. It was organized in 1856 by a combination of voters from other parties for the purpose of opposing the extension of slavery, and in 1860, it elected Abraham Lincoln president.

Sectionalism.

A disproportionate regard for the interests peculiar to a section of the country; local patriotism, as distinguished from national.

Socialism.

A theory or system of social reform which contemplates a complete reconstruction of society, with a more just and equitable division of property and labor. In popular usage, the term is often employed to indicate any lawless, revolutionary social scheme. See Communism, Fourierism, Saint-Simonianism, forms of socialism.

Saint-Simonianism.

The principles, doctrines and practice of the Saint-Simonians.

SAINT-SIMONIAN: A follower of the Count de St. Simon, who died in 1825, and who maintained that the principle of property held in common, and the just division of the fruits of common labor among the members of society, etc., are the true remedy for the social evils which exist.

Toryism.

The principles of the Tories.

TORY: An advocate for royal power.

"The word *Tory* first occurs in English history in 1679, during the struggle in Parliament, occasioned by the introduction of the bill for the exclusion of the Duke of York from the line of succession, and was applied by the advocates of the bill to its opponents as a title of obloquy or contempt. The Tories subsequently took a broader ground, and their leading principle became the maintenance of things as they were. The political successors of the Tories are now commonly known as *Conservatives*."

—*New Am. Cyc.*

Theocracy.

Government of a state by the immediate direction or administration of God; hence, the exercise of political authority by priests, as representing the Deity.

Vandalism.

The spirit or conduct of the Vandals; ferocious cruelty; hostility to the arts and literature, or willful destruction or defacement of their monuments.

VANDAL : One of a Teutonic race, formerly dwelling on the south shore of the Baltic, the most barbarous and fierce of the northern nations that plundered Rome in the fifth century, notorious for destroying the monuments of art and literature. One who willfully destroys or defaces any work of art or literature.

Voluntaryism.

The principles of supporting a religious system and its institutions by voluntary association and effort, rather than by the aid or patronage of the state.

Voodooism.

A degraded form of superstition and sorcery, said to include human sacrifice and cannibalism in some of its rites. It is prevalent among the negroes of Hayti, and to some extent in the United States, and is regarded as a relic of African barbarism.

OLOGIES.

LOGY IS A SUFFIX, AND DENOTES A THEORY; OR DOCTRINE; OR SCIENCE.

THEORETICAL AND SCIENTIFIC:

Aetiology.

The science, doctrine, or demonstration of causes; the science of the origin and development of things.

Agnoiology.

The doctrine concerning those things of which we are necessarily ignorant.

Agriology.

A description or comparative study of savage or uncivilized tribes.

Alethiology.

The science which treats of the nature of truth and evidence.

Amphibology.

A phrase, discourse, or proposition, susceptible of two interpretations; and hence, of uncertain meaning. It differs from *equivocation*, which arises from the twofold sense of a single term.

Angelology.

A discourse on angels, or a body of doctrines in regard to angels. "The same mythology commanded the general consent; the same *angelology*, demonology."—*Milman.*

Anthropology.

1. The science of the structure and functions of the human body.

2. The science of man; sometimes used in a limited sense to mean the study of man as an object of natural history, or as an animal.

3. That manner of expression by which the inspired writers attribute human parts and passions to God.

Anemology.

The doctrine or science of the wind.

Angeology.

The doctrine of the vessels of the human body.

Anthropopathy.

The affections of man, or the application of human passions to the Supreme Being. The ascription of human feelings or passions to God, or to a polytheistic deity.

"In its recoil from the gross *anthropopathy* of the vulgar notions, it falls into the vacuum of absolute apathy."—*Hare*.

"The daring *anthropopathic* imagery by which the prophets often represent God as chiding, upbraiding, threatening."—*Rogers*.

Archeology.

A discourse on antiquity; learning pertaining to antiquity.

Astrology.

The practice or science of predicting events by the aspect or situation of the stars.

Augur.

(Rom. Antiq.) An official diviner who *pretended* to foretell events by the singing, chattering, flight, and feeding of birds, or by signs or omens derived from celestial phenomena, certain appearances of quadrupeds, or unusual occurrences.

> "*Augur* or ill, whose tongue was never found
> Without a priestly curse or boding sound."
> —*Dryden*.

Astrotheology.

Divinity founded on the observation of the heavenly bodies.

Asthenology.

Doctrine of diseases characterized by debility.

Battology.

A needless repetition of words in speaking.

Biology.

The science of life; that branch of knowledge which treats of living matter as distinct from matter which is not living; the study of living tissues. It has to do with the origin, structure, development, function and distribution of animals and plants.

Cetology.

The natural history of the whale and its kindred animals

Chirology.

The art of communicating thoughts by signs with the fingers.

Chiromancy.

The practice of attempting to foretell events or to discover the disposition of a person, by inspecting the lines of the hands.

Chronology.

The science of computing time and ascertaining the date of events.

Conchology.

The doctrine or science of shells.

Cosmology.

The science of the world; description of the world; a treatise relating to the structure and parts of the system of creation, the elements of bodies, the modifications of material things, the laws of motion, and the order and course of nature.

Craniology.

A discourse or treatise on the skull; the science that investigates the structure and use of the skull in relation to intellectual power.

Demonology.

"A discourse or treatise on evil spirits; a treatise on demons; a *supposititious* science which treats of demons and their manifestations."—*Sir W. Scott.*

"The established theology of the heathen world rested upon the basis of *demonism.*"—*Farmer.*

Ecclesiology.

The science of church building and decoration.

Estheticism.

The doctrine of esthetics; esthetic principles; devotion to the beautiful in nature and art.

Euchology.
A formulary of prayers; the book of offices in the Greek Church, containing the liturgy, sacraments, and forms of prayers.

Ethnology.
The science which treats of the division of mankind into races, their origin, distribution and relations, and the peculiarities which characterize them.

Geology.
The science of the structure and materials of the earth.

Gigantology.
An account or description of giants.

Hierology.
The science that treats of the ancient writings and inscriptions of Egyptians.

Horology.
Art of constructing machines for measuring time.

Hydrology.
The science of water, its properties, phenomena, and distribution over the earth's surface.

Ichthyology.
The natural history of fishes; that branch of zoology which relates to fishes, including their structure, classification, and habits.

Iconology.
The doctrine of images.

Meteorology.
The science which treats of the atmosphere and its phenomena, particularly of its variations of heat and moisture, of its winds, storms, etc.

Mineralogy.
The science that treats of minerals, and teaches how to describe, distinguish, and classify them.

Myology.
That part of anatomy which treats of muscles.

Mythology.
A system of fables.

1. The science which treats of myths; a treatise on myths.

2. A body of myths; especially, the collective myths which describe the gods of a heathen people; as, the *Mythology* of the Greeks.

"Imagination has always been, and still is, in a narrow sense, the great *mythologizer*."—*Lowell*.

Necrology.
A register of deaths; an account of the dead.

Neology.
1. The introduction of new words into a language, or a new system of terms.

2. A new doctrine ; especially (Theol.), a doctrine at variance with the received interpretation of revealed truth ; a new method of theological interpretation ; rationalism.

Neurology.
A description of the nerves, and their character.

Noso ogy.
Classification of diseases with their names and definitions.

Numismatology.
The science which treats of coins and medals.

Ontology.
The science of beings. That department of the science of metaphysics which investigates and explains the nature and essential properties and relations of all beings, as such, or the principles and causes of being.

Ophiology.
The history and description of serpents.

Ornithology.
A description of fowls, their forms and habits.

Orology.
The science or description of mountains.

Orthology.
The science that treats of the just description of things.

Osteology.

The science or description of animal bones.

Paleology.

The study or knowledge of antiquities, especially, of prehistoric antiquities ; archæology.

Paleontology.

The science that treats of the ancient life of the earth, or of fossils which are the remains of such life.

Pantology.

A systematic view of all branches of human knowledge ; a work of universal information.

Phrenology.

1. The science of the special functions of the several parts of the brain, or of the supposed connection between the various faculties of the mind and particular organs in the brain.

2. In popular usage, the physiological hypothesis of Gall, that the mental faculties and traits of character are shown on the surface of the head or skull; craniology.

Philology.

The branch of learning that treats of language, its origin, construction, etc. It sometimes includes rhetoric, poetry, history and antiquities.

Phytology.

A treatise on plants, doctrine of plants.

Physiology.

1. The science of the functions of all the different parts or organs of animals or plants.

2. A science of the mind and its various phenomena

Physicotheology.

Theology or divinity illustrated or enforced by physical or natural philosophy.

Pneumatology.

The science of elastic fluid, and of spiritual substances.

Psychology.

The doctrine of the soul, the mind.

"I defined *psychology*, the science conversant about the phenomena of the mind, or conscious subject, or self, or Ego."—*Sir W. Hamilton.*

Pseudology.

Falsehood of speech. A liar is a *Pseudo*.

Pyrology.

That branch of physical science which treats of the properties, phenomena, or effects of heat; also, a treatise on heat.

Pyretology.

"The doctrine of fevers. A discourse or treatise on fevers."—*Hooper*.

Pathognomy.

The science of the passions. The expression of the passions; the science of the signs by which human passions are indicated.

Pharmacology.

The science or art of preparing medicines.

Photology.

The doctrine or science of light; explaining its nature and phenomena; optics.

Phonology.

The science or doctrine of elementary sounds formed by the human voice.

Pabdology.

A mathematical operation by little square rods.

Pathology.

The science of diseases, their causes, etc.

Pantheology.

A system of theology embracing all religions; a complete system of theology.

Somatology.

The doctrine or the science of the general properties of material substances.

Terminology.

The doctrine or explanation of terms.

Toxicology.

A branch of medicine which treats of poisons, their effects, antidotes, and recognition.

Tropology.

A rhetorical mode of speech including tropes.

Uranology.

A discourse or treatise on the heavens and the heavenly bodies; a description of the heavens.

PART II.

MISCELLANY.

Aryan.

1. One of a primitive people supposed to have lived in prehistoric times, in Central Asia, east of the Caspian Sea, and north of the Hindoo Koosh and Paropamisan Mountains; and to have been the stock from which sprang the Hindoo, Persian, Greek, Latin, Celtic, Teutonic, Slavonic, and other races: one of the ethnological divisions of mankind called also Indo-European or Indo-Germanic.

2. The language of the original Aryans (written also Arian).

Art.

1. The employment of means to accomplish some desired end; the adaptation of things in the natural world to the uses of life; the application of knowledge or power to practical purposes.

2. A system of rules serving to facilitate the performance of certain actions; a system of principles and rules for attaining a desired end; method of doing well some especial work; often contradistinguished from *science* or speculative principles; as,

the *art* of building or engraving ; the *art* of war ; the *art* of navigation.

"Science is systematized knowledge ; *art* is knowledge made efficient by skill."—*J. F. Genung.*

3. The application of skill to the production of the beautiful by imitation or design, or an occupation in which skill is so employed, as in painting and sculpture ; one of the fine arts ; as, he prefers *art* to literature.

Analogy.

A resemblance of relations ; an agreement or likeness between things in some circumstances or effects when the things are otherwise entirely different. Thus, learning *enlightens* the mind because it is to the mind, what light is to the eye, enabling it to discover things before hidden.

Analogy is very commonly used to denote similarity or essential resemblance; but its specific meaning is a similarity of *relations*, and in this consists the difference between the argument from *example* and that from *analogy.*

"In the former, we argue from the mere similarity of two things ; in the latter, from the similarity of their relations."—*Karslake.*

Analogism.

Course of reasoning; to think over; to calculate.

"An argument from the cause to the effect; an *a priori* argument."—*Johnson.*

"Investigation of things by the analogy they bear to each other."—*Crabb.*

Anatomism.

The application of the principles of anatomy, as in art.

The doctrine that the anatomical structure explains all the phenomena of the organism or of animal life.

Anthroposcopy.

The art of discovering or judging of a man's character, passions and inclinations from a study of his visible features.

Alienism.

The state of being an alien. That is *alien* that does not belong to the same country, land or government, or to the citizens or subjects thereof; foreign; as, *alien* subjects, enemies, property, shores.

Anthropolatry.

The practice of man worship.

Astrolatry.

The worship of the stars; idolatry.

Atavism.

The recurrence, or a tendency to a recurrence, of the original type of a species in the progeny of its varieties; resemblance to remote rather than to near ancestors; reversion to the original form.

Androgynism.

Union of both sexes in one individual; hermaphroditism.

Anglo-Saxonism.

A characteristic of the Anglo-Saxon race; especially a word or an idiom of the Anglo-Saxon tongue.

Anti-Christ.

A denier or opponent of Christ. A great antagonist, person or power, expected to precede Christ's second coming.

Apologetics.

That branch of theology which defends the Holy Scriptures, and sets forth the evidence of their divine authority.

Africanism.

A word, phrase, idiom, or custom peculiar to Africa or Africans.

Altruism.

Regard for others, both natural and moral; devotion to the interests of others; brotherly kindness, opposed to egoism or selfishness.

Antichronism.

Deviation from the true order of time; anachronism.

Agonism.

Contention for a prize,—a contest.

Athanasian.

The Athanasian creed is an exposition of Christian faith by Athanasius, Bishop of Alexandria.

Atheism.

The disbelief or denial of the existence of a God or supreme intelligent Being.

"*Atheism* is a ferocious system that leaves nothing above us to excite awe, nor around us to awaken tenderness."—*R. Hall.*

"*Atheism* and *pantheism* are often wrongly confounded."—*Shipley.*

Agrarianism.

An equal or equitable division of landed property, the principles or acts of those who favor a redistribution of land; as the Agrarian Sons of Rome, which distributed the conquered and other public lands among the citizens.

Alcoholism.

A diseased condition of the system, brought about by the continued use of alcoholic liquors.

Anachronism.

A misplacing or error in the order of time ; an error in chronology by which events are misplaced in regard to each other, especially one by which an event is placed too early; falsification of chronological relation.

Absenteeism.

"The state or practice of an absentee; especially the practice of absenting one's self from the country or district where his estate is situated ; as, an Irish absentee."—*Macaulay.*

Absinthism.

The condition of being poisoned by the excessive use of absinthe

Absolutism.

The state of being absolute; the system or doctrine of the absolute ; the principles or practice of absolute or arbitrary government ; despotism.

Acrobatism.

Feats of the acrobat; daring gymnastic feats ; high vaulting.

Animalism.

The state, activity or enjoyment of animals ; mere animal life without intellectual or moral qualities ; sensuality.

Animalculism.

The theory which seeks to explain certain physiological and pathological phenomena by means of animalcules.

Atomism.

The doctrine of atoms.

The ATOMIC PHILOSOPHY, or *Doctrine of Atoms*, a system which, assuming that atoms are endued with gravity and motion, accounted thus for the origin and formation of all things. This philosophy was first broached by Leucippus, was developed by Democritus, and afterwards improved by Epicurus, and hence is sometimes denominated the *Epicurean* philosophy.

ATOMIST : One who holds to the atomic philosophy or theory

Averroism.

The tenets of the Averroists.

AVERROIST : One of a sect of peripatetic philosophers who appeared in Italy before the restoration of learning; so denominated from Averroes, or Averrhoes, a celebrated Arabian philosopher. He held the doctrine of monopsychism.

A PERIPATETIC is one who walks about; a pedestrian; an itinerant. The word peripatetic also signifies or pertains to the philosophy taught by Aristotle (who gave his instructions while walking in the Lyceum at Athens) ; or to his followers. "The true *peripatetic* school."—*Howell.*

Bacchanalianism.

The practice of Bacchanalians; bacchanals; drunken revelry.

BACCHANAL :

1. A devotee of Bacchus ; one who indulges in drunken revels.

2. The festival of Bacchus ; the bacchanalia.

3. A song or a dance in honor of Bacchus.

Barbarism.

Savageness ; ignorance; impropriety of speech ; an uncivilized state.

Burkism.

Practice of killing persons for the purpose of selling the bodies for dissection.

Baptist.

1. One who administers baptism ;—specifically applied to John the forerunner of Christ.

2. One of a denomination of Christians who deny the validity of infant baptism, and of sprinkling, and maintain that baptism should be administered to believers alone, and should be by immersion.

Cynicism.

A morose contempt of the pleasures and acts of life.

CYNIC: One of a sect or school of philosophers founded by Anthisthenes, and of whom Diogenes was a disciple. The first Cynics were noted for austere lives and their scorn for social customs and current philosophical opinions. Hence the term Cynic symbolized, in the popular judgment, moroseness and contempt for the views of others.

Cardinal Virtues.

These are Prudence; Justice; Temperance; **and** Fortitude.

Certainties.

The immutable and undeviating laws of nature.

MORAL CERTAINTIES are such as are supported by the evidence of reason or probability. Its opposites are physical and mathematical certainties.

THE SENSES: These are the five animal senses—as seeing; hearing; feeling; tasting; smelling. To these may be added the moral senses, that is, the sense of right and wrong, common to all, and conscience.

Casuistry.

1. The science or doctrine of dealing with cases of conscience, of resolving questions of right or

wrong in conduct, or of determining the lawfulness or unlawfulness of what a man may do, by rules and principles drawn from the Scriptures, from the laws of society or the church, or from equity and natural reason; the application of general moral rules to particular cases.

"The consideration of these nice and puzzling questions in the science of ethics has given rise, in modern times, to a particular department of it, distinguished by the title of casuistry."—*Stewart.*

2. "*Casuistry* is the science of cases (*i. e.*, oblique deflections from the general rule)."—*DeQuincey.*

Christian Science.

The doctrine that FAITH and PRAYER alone are all sufficient to remove or cure any and all diseases that torment or afflict the human body; that where FAITH and PRAYER cannot avail, *materia medica* and a physician must fail. A MISUSE and ABUSE of the words Christian and Science.

Charlatanism.

Undue pretensions to skill; quackery; wheedling; empiricism.

Cliquism.

A tendency to associate in cliques; the spirit of cliques.

Conceptualism.

A theory; intermediate between realism and nominalism, that the mind has the power of forming for itself general conceptions of individual or single objects.

Criticism.

1. The rules and principles which regulate the practice of the critic; the art of judging with knowledge and propriety of the beauties and faults of a literary performance, or of a production in the fine arts; as, dramatic *criticism*.

Crusade.

1. Any one of the military expeditions undertaken by Christian powers, in the eleventh, twelfth and thirteenth centuries, for the recovery of the Holy Land from the Mohammedans.

2. Any enterprise undertaken with zeal and enthusiasm; as, a *crusade* against intemperance.

> "Azure-eyed and golden-haired,
> Forth the young *crusaders* fared."
>
> —*Longfellow*.

Death.

The cessation of life. The ceasing to exist.

An ingenious theory as to the cause of death has been brought forward by Philip, in his work on "Sleep and Death," in which he claims that to the highest form of life three orders of functions are necessary, viz.: the muscular, nervous, and sensorial; that of these the two former are independent of the latter, and continue in action for a while after its cessation; that they might thus continue always, but for the fact that they are dependent on the process of respiration; that this process is a voluntary act, depending upon the will, and that the latter is embraced in the sensorial function. In this view, death is the suspension or removal of the sensorial function, and that leads to the suspension of the others through the cessation of respiration. —*Philip. Sleep and Death ; Dean, Med. Jur. 413 et seq.*

Doctrine.

1. Teaching; instruction.

He taught them many things by parables, and said unto them in his *doctrine*, Hearken.—*Mark iv. 2.*

2. That which is taught; what is held, put forth as true, and supported by a teacher, a school, or a sect; a principle or position, or the body of principles, in any branch of knowledge; any tenet or dogma; a principle of faith; as, the *doctrine* of

atoms; the *doctrine* of chances; the *doctrine* of gravitation.

The Monroe Doctrine (Politics), a policy enunciated by President Monroe (Message, Dec. 2, 1823), the essential feature of which is that the United States will regard as an unfriendly act any attempt on the part of European powers to extend their system on this continent, or any interference to oppress, or in any manner control the destiny of governments whose independence has been acknowledged by the United States.

Syn.—Precept; tenet; principle; maxim; dogma. DOCTRINE, PRECEPT. *Doctrine* denotes whatever is recommended as a speculative truth to the belief of others. *Precept* is a rule laid down to be obeyed. *Doctrine* supposes a teacher; *Precept* supposes a superior, with a right to command. The *doctrines* of the Bible; the *precepts* of our holy religion.

Dogma.

1. That which is held as an opinion; a tenet; a doctrine.

2. A formally stated and authoritatively settled doctrine; a definite, established, and authoritative tenet.

3. A doctrinal notion asserted without regard to evidence or truth; an arbitrary dictum.

Syn.—Tenet; opinion; proposition; doctrine.

DOGMA, TENET. A TENET is that which is maintained as true with great firmness; as the tenets of our holy religion.

A DOGMA is that which is laid down with authority as indubitably true, especially a religious doctrine; as, the dogmas of the church. A *tenet* rests on its own intrinsic merits or demerits; a *dogma* rests on an authority regarded as competent to decide and determine.

Demonolatry.

The worship of demons.

Darwinism.

The theory or doctrines put forth by Darwin.

DARWINIAN: Pertaining to Darwin; as, the Darwinian theory.

This theory was put forth by Darwin in 1859 in a work entitled, "The Origin of Species by Means of Natural Selection." The author argues that, in the struggle for existence, those creatures best fitted to the requirements of the situation in which they are placed are the ones that will live; in other words, that Nature selects those which are to survive. This is the theory of *natural selection* or the *survival of the fittest*. He also argues that natural selection is capable of modifying and producing organisms fit for their circumstances.

Dilettanteism.

The state or quality of being a *dilettante ;* the desultory pursuit of art, science, or literature.

DILETTANTE : An admirer or lover of the fine arts; popularly, an amateur; especially, one who follows an art or a branch of knowledge desultorily, or for amusement only.

Evolution Theory.

The evolution or development theory declares the universe as it now exists to be the result of a long series of changes, which were so far related to each other as to form a series of growths analogous to the evolving of the parts of a growing organism. Herbert Spencer defines evolution as a progress from the homogeneous to the heterogeneous, from general to special, from the simple to the complex elements of life; and it is believed that this process can be traced to the formation of worlds in space, in the multiplication of types and species among animals and plants, in the origin and changes of languages and literature and the arts, and also in all changes of human institutions and society. Asserting the general fact of progress in nature, the evolution theory shows that the method of this progress has been (1) by the multiplication of organs and functions; (2) according to a defined unity of plan, although with (3) the intervention of transitional forms, and (4) with modifications dependent upon surrounding conditions. Ancient writers occasionally seemed to have a glimmering knowledge of the fact of progress in nature, but as a theory "evolution" belongs to the enlightenment of the nineteenth century. Leibnitz, in the latter part of the seventeenth century, first uttered the opinion that the earth was once in a fluid condition, and Kant, about the middle of the eighteenth century, definitely propounded the nebular hypothesis, which was enlarged to a theory by the Herschels. The first writer to suggest the transmutation of species among animals was Buffon, about 1750, and other writers followed out the idea. The eccentric Lord Monboddo was the first to suggest the possible descent of man from the ape about 1774. In 1813 Dr. W. C. Wells first proposed to apply the principle of natural selection to the natural history of man, and in 1822 Professor Herbert first asserted the probable transmutation of species of plants. In 1844 a book appeared called "Vestiges of Creation," which, though evidently not written by a scientific student, yet attracted great attention by its bold and ingenious theories. The authorship of this book was never revealed until after the death of Robert Chambers, a few years since; it became known that this publisher, whom no one would ever have suspected of holding such heterodox theories, had actually written it. But the two great apostles of the evolution theory were Charles Darwin and Herbert Spencer. The latter began his great work, the "First Principles of Philosophy," showing the application of evolution in the facts of life, in 1852. In 1859 appeared Darwin's "Origin of Species." The hypothesis of the latter was that different species originated in spontaneous variation, and the survival of the fittest through natural selection and the struggle for existence. This theory was further elaborated and applied by Spencer, Darwin, Huxley, and other writers in Europe and America, and though to-day by no means all of the ideas upheld by these early advocates of the theory are still accepted, evolution as a principle is now acknowledged by nearly all scientists. It is taken to be an established fact in nature, a valid induction from man's knowledge of natural order.

Empiricism.

1. The method or practice of an empiric; pursuit of knowledge by observation and experiment.

2. Specifically, a practice of medicine founded on mere experience, without the aid of science or a knowledge of principles; ignorant and unscientific practice; charlatanry; quackery.

3. (Metaph.) The philosophical theory which attributes the origin of all our knowledge to experience

Eclecticism.

Theory or practice of an eclectic.

ECLECTIC : One who follows an eclectic method; selecting; choosing (what is true or excellent in doctrines, opinions, etc.), from various sources or systems ; as, an *eclectic* philosopher ; an *eclectic* physician who selects his mode of practice and medicines from all schools.

Egoism.

1. The doctrine of certain extreme adherents or disciples of Descartes and Johann Gottlieb Fichte, which finds all the elements of knowledge in the

ego and the relations which it implies or provides for.

Eleaticism.

The Eleatic doctrine.

ELEATIC : Of or pertaining to a certain school of Greek philosophers, who taught that the only certain science is that which owes nothing to the senses, and all to the reason.

Externalism.

1. The quality of being manifest to the senses; external acts or appearances; regard for externals.

2. That philosophy or doctrine which recognizes or deals only with externals, or objects of sense—perception; positivism; phenomenalism

Experientialism.

The doctrine that experience, either that of ourselves or of others, is the test or criterion of general knowledge; opposed to intuitionalism.

Epicureanism.

Indulgence in luxury, voluptuousness.

Eudemonism.

That system of ethics which defines and enforces moral obligation by its relation to happiness or personal well-being.

Euhemerism.

The theory, held by Euhemerus, that the gods of mythology were but deified mortals, and their deeds only the amplification in imagination of human acts.

Etherealism.

The state of being ethereal; etherealness.

ETHER: (Physics) A medium of great elasticity and extreme tenuity, *supposed* to pervade all space, the interior of solid bodies not excepted, and to be the medium of transmission of light and heat; hence often called *luminiferous ether*.

2. Supposed matter above the air; the air itself

3. A medium of communication. "*Etherealized,* moreover, by spiritual communications with the other world."—*Hawthorne.*

Fate of the Apostles.

The following brief history of the fate of the Apostles may be new to those whose reading has not been evangelical:

St. Matthew is supposed to have suffered martyrdom or was slain with the sword at the city of Ethiopia.

St. Mark was dragged through the streets of Alexandria, in Egypt, till he expired.

St. Luke was hanged upon an olive tree in Greece.

St. John was put into a caldron of boiling oil at Rome and escaped death. He afterward died a natural death at Ephesus in Asia.

St. James the Great was beheaded at Jerusalem.

St. James the Less was thrown from a pinnacle or wing of the Temple and then beaten to death with a fuller's club.

St. Philip was hanged up against a pillar at Hieropolis, a city of Phrygia.

St. Bartholomew was flayed alive by the command of a barbarous king.

St. Andrew was bound to a cross, whence he preached unto the people till he expired.

St. Thomas was run through the body with a lance at Caromandel, in the East Indies.

St. Jude was shot to death with arrows.

St. Simon Zelotes was crucified in Persia.

St. Matthias was first stoned and then beheaded.

St. Barnabas was stoned to death by Jews at Salania.

St. Paul was beheaded at Rome by the tyrant Nero.

Faith.

1. Belief; the assent of the mind to the truth of what is declared by another, resting on his authority and veracity.

2. The assent of the mind to the truth of a proposition advanced by another.

3. *In theology*, the assent of the mind to the truth of what God has revealed.

4. The object of belief; the doctrines or system of doctrines believed.

5. Fidelity; sincerity; faithfulness; honor.

Fabian.

Of, pertaining to, or in the manner of, the Roman general, Quintus Fabius Maximus Verrucous; cautious; dilatory; avoiding a decisive contest.

FABIAN POLICY: A policy like that of Fabius Maximus, who, by carefully avoiding decisive contests, foiled Hannibal, harassing his army by marches, countermarches, and ambuscades; a policy of delays and cautions.

Gyneolatry.

The worship of women.

"The sentimental gyneolatry of chivalry, which was at best but skin-deep."—*Lowell.*

Helot.

A slave in ancient Sparta.

HELOTISM: The slavery of the Helots.

"Those unfortunates, the *Helots* of mankind, more or less numerous in every community."—*J. Taylor.*

Hagiolatry.

The invocation or worship of the saints.

Heliolatry.

That species of idolatry which consists in worshiping the sun, moon and stars.

Humanism.

The study of the humanities; polite learning.

HUMANIST: One of the scholars who in the field of literature proper represented the movement of the Renaissance, and early in the sixteenth century adopted the name *Humanist* as their distinctive title.

"She looked almost like a being who had rejected with indifference the attitude of sex for the loftier quality of abstract *humanism.*"—*Hardy.*

Iconoclasm.

The doctrine or practice of the iconoclasts; image breaking.

Iconoclast.

1. A breaker or destroyer of idols or images; a determined enemy of idol worship.

2. One who exposes or destroys impositions or shams; one who attacks cherished beliefs; a radical.

Iconolatry.

The worship of images as symbols.

Ignis fatuus.

A meteor that appears in the night over marshy grounds, supposed to be occasioned by phosphoric matter, extracted from putrefying animal or vegetable substances, called WILL WITH THE WISP, or JACK WITH A LANTERN.

Judaism.

The tenets and rights of the Jews.

SENTIMENTS OF THE JEWS:—1. That God is the creator of all things; that he guides and supports all creatures; that he has done everything; and that he still acts, and shall act during the whole of eternity. 2. That God is one; there is no unity like his. He alone hath been, is, and shall be eternally one God. 3. That God is incorporeal, and cannot have any material properties; and no corporeal essence can be compared with him. 4. That God is the beginning and end of all things, and shall eternally subsist. 5. That God alone ought to be worshiped, and none beside him is to be adored. 6. That whatever has been taught by the prophets is true. 7. That Moses is the head and father of all temporary doctors (teachers), of those who lived before, or shall live after him. 8. That the law was given by Moses. 9. That the law shall never be altered, and that God will give no other. 10. That God knows all the thoughts and actions of men. 11. That God will regard the works of all those who have performed what he commands, and punish those who have transgressed his law. 12. That the Messiah is to come, though he tarry a long time. 13. That there shall be a resurrection of the dead when God shall see fit.

Life.

"Life is the substance of the forces by which death is resisted."—*Bichat*.

A state in which energy and function is ever resisting decay and dissolution.

Legend.

Any wonderful story coming down from the past, but not *verifiable* by historical record; a myth; a fable.

Method.

1. " An orderly procedure or process; regular manner of doing anything; hence, manner; way; mode; as, a *method* of teaching languages; a *method* of improving the mind."—*Addison.*

2. Orderly arrangement, elucidation, development, or classification; clear and lucid exhibition; systematic arrangement peculiar to an individual.

"Though this be madness, yet there's *method* in it."
—*Shakespeare.*

"All *method* is a rational process, a progress toward an end."—*Sir W. Hamilton.*

Syn.—Order; system; rule; regularity; way; manner; mode; course; process; means.

METHOD, MODE, MANNER. *Method* implies arrangement; *mode*, mere action or existence. *Method* is a way of reaching a given end by a *series* of acts which tend to secure it; *mode* relates to a single action, or to the form which a series of acts, viewed as a whole, exhibits. *Manner* is literally the *handling* of a thing, and has a wider sense, embracing both *method* and *mode*. An instructor may adopt a good *method* of teaching to write; the scholar may acquire a bad *mode* of holding his pen; the *manner* in which he is corrected will greatly affect his success or failure.

Magic.

A comprehensive name for all of the pretended arts which claim to produce effects by the assistance of supernatural beings, or departed spirits, or by a mastery of secret forces in nature attained by a study of occult science, including enchantment, conjuration, witchcraft, sorcery, necromancy, incantation, etc.

"An appearance made by some magic."—*Chaucer*.

CELESTIAL MAGIC, a supposed supernatural power which gave to spirits a kind of dominion over the *planets*, and to the *planets* an influence over men. Natural magic, the art of employing the powers of nature to produce effects apparently supernatural.

SUPERSTITIONS, or GEOTIC, magic, the invocation of devils or demons, involving the supposition of some tacit or express agreement between them and human beings.

Monism.

That doctrine which refers all phenomena to a single ultimate constituent or agent; the opposite of *dualism*.

The doctrine has been held in three generic forms; matter and its phenomena have been explained as a modification of mind, involving an idealistic *monism;* or mind has been explained by and resolved into matter, giving a materialistic *monism;* or, thirdly, matter, mind, and their phenomena have been held to be manifestations or modifications of some one substance, like a substance of Spinoza, or a supposed unknown something of some evolutionists, which is capable of an objective and subjective aspect.

Mariolatry.
The worship of the Virgin Mary.

Moravianism.
The religious system of the Moravians.

Mesmerism.
The art of communicating a species of sleep which is supposed to affect the body while the mind or intellectual power is active and intelligent.

Mountebank.
A stage doctor, a false pretender.

Memnon.
An Egyptian statue, supposed to emit musical sounds at sunrise.

Memento mori.
Be mindful of death.

Memorabilia.

Things worthy to be remembered.

Miracle.

An act or event beyond the ordinary laws of nature; a wonder. In theology, an event contrary to the established course of things, or a deviation from the known laws of nature; a supernatural event.

Mirage.

An optical effect, sometimes seen on the ocean, but more frequently in deserts, due to total reflection of light at the surface common to two strata of air differently heated. The reflected image is seen, commonly in an inverted position, while the real object may or may not be in sight. When the surface is horizontal, and below the eye, the appearance is that of a sheet of water in which the object is seen reflected; when the reflecting surface is above the eye, the image is seen projected against the sky. The *fata morgana* and *looming* are species of *mirage*.

"By the *mirage* uplifted the land floats vague in the ether,
Ships and the shadows of ships hang in motionless air."
—*Longfellow.*

Nominalism.

Words, not things, are the object of dialectics. The principles or philosophy of the Nominalists.

NOMINALIST: One of a sect of philosophers in the Middle Ages, who adopted the opinion of Roscelin, that general conceptions, or universals, exist in name only.

Nick.

In northern mythology an evil spirit of the waters.

Necrolatry.

The worship of the dead ; manes worship.

Optimism.

The doctrine that everything is for the best, or that the order of things in the universe is adapted to produce the most good.

Ostracism.

Banishment by votes on shells ; banishment by the voice of the populace.

Pythian.

Pertaining to Pythia, the priestess of Apollo

Pythoness.

A priestess who gave oracular answers at Delphi in Greece.

Physiolatry.

The worship of the powers or agencies of nature's materialism in religion · nature worship.

Pauperism.

State of indigence requiring maintenance for the poor ; state of being poor.

Petalism.

Banishment by writing a vote on a leaf.

Pessimism.

The opinion or doctrine that everything in nature is ordered for or tends to the worst ; or that the world is wholly evil ; opposed to optimism.

Parseeism.

The religion of the Parsees ; followers of Zoroaster.

Parasitism

The manners of a parasite, a hanger-on, a fawning flatterer of the rich.

Pharisaism.

1. The notions, doctrines and conduct of the Pharisees, as a sect.

2. Rigid observance of external forms of religion, without genuine piety ; hypocrisy in religion ; a

censorious, self-righteous spirit in matters of morals or manners.

PHARISEE: One of a sect or party among the Jews, noted for a strict and formal observance of rites and ceremonies and of the traditions of the elders, and whose pretensions to superior sanctity led them to separate themselves from the other Jews.

Phenomenon.

1. An appearance; anything visible; whatever, in matter or spirit, is apparent to, or is apprehended by, observation; as, the *phenomena* of heat, light, or electricity; *phenomena* of imagination or memory.

2. That which strikes one as strange, unusual, or unaccountable; an extraordinary or very remarkable person, thing, or occurrence; as, a musical phenomena.

Psychical.

Of or pertaining to the human soul, or to the living principle in man.

"This term was formerly used to express the same idea as *psychological*. Recent metaphysicians, however, have employed it to mark the difference between the living principle in man and the rational or spiritual part of his nature. In this use the word describes the human soul in its relation to sense, appetite and the outer visible world, as distinguished from spiritual or rational faculties, which have to do with the supersensible world."—*Heyse*.

PSYCHE: The soul; the vital principle; the mind.

Parthenon.
A celebrated Grecian temple of Minerva.

Proselytism.
The making of converts.

Provincialism.
Peculiarity of speech in a province or district remote from the metropolis.

Purism.
Immaculate morals and conduct.

Putanism.
Customary lewdness.

Pantheon.
The temple in Rome dedicated to all the deities.

Pandemonium.
The council hall of fallen angels.

Pythonism.
The art of predicting events after the manner of the priestess of Apollo at Delphi; equivocal prophesying.

Quidnunc.

One curious to know everything.

Quixotism.

Romantic and absurd notions. That form of delusion that leads to extravagant and absurd undertakings or sacrifices in obedience to a morbidly romantic ideal of duty or honor, as illustrated by the exploits of Don Quixote in knight-errantry.

Rhapsody.

Unconnected writing or discourse

Rabbi.

A Jewish doctor. This title is not conferred by authority but allowed by courtesy to learned men.

RABBINIC: The language of the Rabbins.

Rabbinism.

A rabbinic expression.

RABBINIST: One who adhered to the Talmud. The body of the Jewish civil and canonical law not comprised in the Pentateuch.

Realism.

1. As opposed to Nominalism, the doctrine that genera and species are real things or entities, existing independently of our conceptions. According to

Realism the universal exists ante rem (Plato), or in re (Aristotle).

2. As opposed to idealism, the doctrine that in sense perception, there is an immediate cognition of the external object and our knowledge of it is not mediate and representative.

3. The doctrine of the Realists, who maintain that things, not words, are the objects of dialectics, the opposite of Nominalism.

Religion.

A system of faith and worship.

Rosicrucians.

A sect of philosophers who in the fourteenth century made great pretensions to science.

Science.

1. Knowledge; knowledge of principles and causes; ascertained truth or facts.

2. Accumulated and established knowledge, which has been systematized and formulated with reference to the discovery of general truths or the operation of general laws; knowledge classified and made available in work, life, or the search for truth; comprehensive, profound, or philosophical knowledge.

3. Especially, such knowledge when it relates to the physical world and its phenomena, the nature, constitution, and forces of matter, the qualities and functions of living tissues, etc., called also *natural science*, and *physical science*.

Syn.—Literature ; art ; knowledge.

SCIENCE, LITERATURE, ART. *Science* is literally *knowledge*, but more usually denotes a systematic and orderly arrangement of knowledge. In a more distinctive sense, *science* embraces those branches of knowledge of which the subject-matter is either ultimate principles, or facts as explained by principles or laws thus arranged in natural order. The term *literature* sometimes denotes all compositions not embraced under *science* but is usually confined to the *belles-lettres*. *Art* is that which depends on practice and skill in performance. "In *science, scimus ut sciamus;* in *art, scimus ut producamus*. And, therefore, *science* and *art* may be said to be investigation of truth ; but one, *science*, inquires for the sake of knowledge ; the other, *art*, for the sake of production ; and hence *science* is more concerned with the higher truths, *art* with the lower ; and *science* never is engaged, as *art* is, in productive application. And the most perfect state of *science*, therefore, will be the most high and accurate inquiry; the perfection of *art* will be the most apt and efficient system of rules; art always throwing itself into the form of rules."—*Karslake.*

Syllogism.

An argument of three propositions, of which the two first are called the premises, and the last the conclusion.

Syncretism.

A mixture in philosophy or religion.

System.

Connection of parts or things; a whole connected scheme.

Savagism.

State of man in native rudeness.

Scampism.

Among the Persians, a mode of punishment by confining a criminal in a hollow tree till he dies.

Scholasticism.

The method or subtleties of the schools of philosophy; scholastic formality; scholastic doctrines or philosophy

Scoundrelism.

Baseness, turpitude, rascality.

Sensationalism.

1. The doctrine held by Condillac, and by some ascribed to Locke, that our ideas originate solely in sensation, and consist of sensations transformed; sensualism; opposed to rationalism, and intuitionalism.

2. The practice or methods of sensational writing or speaking; as, the sensationalism of a novel.

Sciolism.

Superficial knowledge.

SCIOLIST: One who knows little, or who knows many things superficially.

Sensualism.

The doctrine that all our ideas, or the operations of the understanding, not only originate in sensation, but are transformed.

Schism.

In a general sense, division, or separation; but appropriately, a division or separation in the church.

Somatist.

One who denies the existence of spiritual substances.

Stoical.

Those who affect insensibility to pain, mental or bodily.

Superstition.

1. An excessive reverence for, or fear of, that which is unknown or mysterious.

2. An ignorant or irrational worship of the Supreme Deity; excessive exactness or rigor in religious opinions or practice; extreme and unnecessary scruples in the observance of religious rites not commanded, or of points of minor importance; also, a rite or practice proceeding from excess of scruples in religion.

3. The worship of a false god or gods; false religion; religious veneration for unworthy objects.

4. Belief in the direct agency of superior powers in certain extraordinary or singular events, or in magic, omens, prognostics, or the like.

Syn.—Fanaticism. SUPERSTITION, FANATICISM. *Superstition* springs from religious feeling, misdirected or unenlightened. *Fanaticism* arises from this same feeling in a state of high-wrought and self-confident excitement. The former leads in some cases to excessive rigor in religious opinions or practice, in others, to unfounded belief in extraordinary events or in charms, omens, and prognostics, hence producing weak fears, or excessive scrupulosity as to outward observances. The latter gives rise to an utter disregard of reason under the false assumption of enjoying a guidance directly inspired. *Fanaticism* has a secondary sense as applied to Politics, etc., which corresponds to the primary.

The Seven Bibles of the World

Are the Koran of the Mohammedans, the Eddas of the Scandinavians, the Try Pitikes of the Buddhists, the Five Kings of the Chinese, the Three Vedas of the Hindoos, the Zendavesta, and the Scriptures of the Christians. The Koran is the most recent of these seven Bibles, and not older than the seventh century of our era. It is a compound of quotations from the Old and New Testament, the Talmud, and the Gospel of St. Barnabas. The Eddas of the Scandinavians were first published in the fourteenth century. The Pitikes of the Buddhists contain sublime morals and pure aspirations, and their author lived and died in the sixth century before Christ. There is nothing of excellence in these sacred books not found in the Bible. The sacred writings of the Chinese are called the Five Kings, king meaning web of cloth, or the warp that keeps the threads in place. They contain the best sayings of the best sages on the ethico-political duties of life. These sayings cannot be traced to a period higher than the eleventh century before Christ. The Three Vedas are the most ancient books of the Hindoos, and it is the opinion of Max Muller, Wilson, Johnson and Whitney that they are not older than eleven centuries before Christ. The Zendavesta of the Persians is the grandest of all sacred books next to our Bible. Zoroaster, whose sayings it contains, was born in the twelfth century before Christ. Moses lived and wrote his Pentateuch fifteen centuries before Christ, and, therefore, has a clear margin of three hundred years older than the most ancient of the sacred writings.—*Little Giant Cyc.*

Traditionalism.

A system of faith founded on tradition, especially the doctrine that all religious faith is to be based solely upon what is delivered from competent authority, exclusive of rational processes.

TRADITION: 1. The unwritten or oral delivery of information, opinions, doctrines, practices, rites, customs, from father to son, or from ancestors to posterity ; the transmission of any knowledge, opinions, or practice, from forefathers to descendants by oral communication, without written memorials.

2. (Theol.) An unwritten code of law represented to have been given by God to Moses on Sinai.

3. That body of doctrine and discipline, or any article thereof, supposed to have been put forth by Christ or his apostles, and not committed to writing.

"Stand fast, and hold the *traditions* which ye have been taught, whether by word, or our epistle."—*II Thess. ii. 15.*

Theology.

The science of God or of religion ; the science that treats of the existence, character and attributes of God, his laws and government, the doctrines we are to believe, and the duties we are to practice ; divinity ; the knowledge derived from the Scriptures, the systematic exhibition of revealed truth, the science of Christian faith and life.

"Many speak of *theology* as a science of religion (instead of science of God) because they disbelieve that there is any knowledge of God to be attained." —*Prof. R. Flint (Enc. Brit.)*

"Theology is ordered knowledge representing in the region of the intellect what religion represents in the heart and life of man."—*Gladstone.*

ASCETIC THEOLOGY, the science which treats of the practice of theological and moral virtue, and the counsels of perfection.

NATURAL THEOLOGY, or NATURAL RELIGION, is that part of theological science which treats of those evidences of the existence and attributes of the Supreme Being which are exhibited in nature;—distinguished from REVEALED RELIGION.

"I call that *Natural* religion which men might know by the mere principles of reason, improved by consideration and experience, without the help of revelation."—*Bishop Wilkins.*

MORAL THEOLOGY, that phase of theology which is concerned with moral character and conduct.

REVEALED THEOLOGY: Theology which is to be learned only from revelation.

SCHOLASTIC THEOLOGY: Theology as taught by the scholastics, or as prosecuted after their principles and methods.

SPECULATIVE THEOLOGY: Theology as founded upon, or influenced by speculation or metaphysical philosophy.

SYSTEMATIC THEOLOGY: That branch of theology of which the aim is to reduce all revealed truth to a series of statements that together shall constitute an organized whole.—*Robinson* (*Johnson's Cyc.*)

The Mind Cure.

The mind cure, otherwise known in its various subdivisions as metaphysics, Christian science, mental science, etc., is a species of delusion quite popular at the present time. Every era of the world has cherished similar delusions, for the mass of the human race, even in what are considered the educated classes, are so unfamiliar with the processes of exact reasoning that they fall a ready prey to quacks of all kinds. The fundamental idea of the mind cure system is that there is no such thing as sickness. Disease, says one of their apostles, is an error of the mind, the result of fear. Fear is only faith inverted and perverted. God, who is all good himself, and who made everything good, cannot have been the author of any disease. As disease, therefore, is not a creation, it has no existence, and when the healer has succeeded in impressing this fact upon the mind of the patient, the cure is effected. It is curious to note into what utter absurdities the need for consistency carries these apostles. Poisons, they say, would be quite harmless if the fear of them was removed, but we have yet to find the "mental science" teacher who will undertake to prove this by herself taking liberal doses of aconite and strychnine. The illnesses of children are explained by the hypothesis of hereditary fear. The majority of the teachers of this new faith are women, many of whom, no doubt, are sincere in their belief; but it may be safely stated that the men engaged as the so-called physicians of the new practice are, with few exceptions, unprincipled quacks, who have gone into the business for the money they can make by duping the ignorant. As far as there is any truth underlying the vagaries of mind cures, and their boasts of remarkable cases of healing, it may be admitted that the mind has much influence over the body. This fact has been recognized by intelligent physicians for centuries. And that the peculiar modern type of nervous diseases, which are so largely caused by excessive stimulus of the nerves and imagination, should be amenable to cure through the imagination, is not strange. It will be noted that this mental cure has effected its miracles mainly among women, where it has the emotional temperament to work on, and almost wholly in the ranks of the wealthy and well-to-do, where there is little or no impoverishment of the system by insufficient food and excessive toil to hinder its effects. We have not heard, nor are we likely to hear, of any epidemic disease checked by the mind cure, or of the healing of acute affections or organic troubles through its agency. Nor do we hear of its seeking to carry its message of healing into the houses of the suffering poor in large cities, where hunger, exposure and foul airs open wide the door to fevers and all deadly diseases, nor yet into hospitals for contagious or incurable affections. In the presence of such realities it would prove, as its votaries probably understand, a too painful mockery. Intelligently analyzed, therefore, this new revelation amounts to nothing more than a quite striking proof of the remarkable influence of the mind over the nervous system. Beyond this, the craze, in attempting to disprove the existence of disease, and to show that poisons do not kill, is simply running against the plain and inevitable facts of life, and can safely be left to perish through its own rashness.

The Bible.

There is no date from beginning to end in the Bible. It comprises some sixty documents and is supposed to have been written by about forty men. Fifty-four miracles are recorded in the Old and fifty-one in the New Testament. Total, one hundred and five.—*Little Giant Cyc.*

Theory.

1. A doctrine, or scheme of things, which terminates in speculation or contemplation, without a view to practice ; hypothesis ; speculation.

"This word is employed by English writers in a very loose and improper sense. It is with them usually convertible into *hypothesis*, and *hypothesis* is commonly used as another term for *conjecture*. The terms *theory* and *theoretical* are properly used in opposition to the terms *practice* and *practical*. In this sense, they were exclusively employed by the ancients ; and in this sense, they are almost exclusively employed by the Continental philosophers."—*Sir W. Hamilton.*

2. An exposition of the general or abstract principles of any science ; as, the *theory* of music.

3. The science, as distinguished from the art ; as, the *theory* and practice of medicine.

4. The philosophical explanation of phenomena, either physical or moral ; as, Lavoisier's *theory* of

combustion; Adam Smith's *theory* of moral sentiments.

5. A *theory* is a scheme of the relations subsisting between the parts of a systematic whole; an *hypoth esis* is a tentative conjecture respecting a cause or phenomena.

Theurgy.

1. A divine work; a miracle; hence, magic; sorcery.

2. "A kind of magical science or art developed in Alexandria among the Neophatonists, and supposed to enable man to influence the will of the gods by means of purification and other sacramental rites."— *Schaff-Herzog Encyc.*

3. In later or modern magic, that species of magic in which effects are claimed to be produced by *supernatural* agency, in distinction from *natural* magic.

Tribalism.

The state of existing in tribes, also, tribal feeling; tribal prejudice or exclusiveness, tribal peculiarities or characteristics.

Themis.

In the mythology of the Greeks—the Goddess of Justice.

Tantalism.

"A punishment like that of Tantalus ; a teasing or tormenting by the hope or near approach of good which is not attainable."—*Addison.*

Talmud.

The book of Hebrew Traditions, laws, and explanations.

Truism.

An undoubted or self-evident truth ; a statement which is plainly true ; a proposition needing no proof or argument ; opposed to *falsism.*

Ultraism.

The principles of men who advocate extreme measures

Utopia.

A term invented by Sir Thomas More, from the Greek word, meaning, no place, and applied to an imaginary isle, which he represents as enjoying the greatest perfection in politics, laws, etc., hence, ideal, chimerical.

Vernacularism.

A vernacular idiom, belonging to the country of one's birth; belonging to the person by birth or nature.

Ventriloquism.

The art or practice of speaking so that the voice seems to come from a distance.

Vulgarism.

A vulgar expression.

Worship.

Religious homage and service. To worship is to perform acts of adoration; to perform religious service; to pay divine honor.

Witticism.

A sentence or phrase affectedly witty.

Whigism.

The principles of Whigs; a friend to free government, one opposed to Tories.

Zymology.

The doctrine of fermentation of liquors.

Zoology.

That part of natural history which treats of the structure, habits, classification, etc., of all animals.

DIVINATION.

Divination is the art of divining; a foreseeing or foretelling of future events; the pretended art of discovering secret or future things by preternatural means.

There shall not be found among you any one that . . . . useth *divination*, or an observer of times, or an enchanter.—Deut. xviii : 10.

Among the ancient heathen philosophers *natural* divination was supposed to be effected by a divine affilitus ; *artificial* divination by certain rites, omens, or appearances, as the flight of birds, entrials of animals, etc.

Aeromancy.
Divination by means of the air and wind.

Anthracomancy.
Divination by inspecting a burning coal.

Anthropomancy.
Divination by the entrails of a human being.

Aruspicy.
Prognostication by inspection of the entrails of victims slain in sacrifice.

Astragalomancy.

Divination by means of small bones or dice.

Austromancy.

Soothsaying or prediction of events, from observation of the winds.

Axinomancy.

A species of divination by means of an ax or hatchet.

Alectryomancy.

Divination by means of a cock and grains of corn placed on the letters of the alphabet, the letters being put together in the order in which the grains were eaten.

Aleuromancy.

Divination by means of flour.

Alomancy.

Divination by means of salt.

Alphitomancy.

Divination by means of barley meal.

Aeromancy.

Divination from the state of the air or from atmospheric substances; also, forecasting changes in the weather.

Belomancy.

A kind of divination anciently practiced by means of marked arrows drawn at random from a bag or quiver, the marks on the arrows drawn being supposed to foreshow the future.

Bibliomancy.

A kind of divination, performed by selecting passages of Scripture at hazard, and drawing from them indications concerning future events.

Capnomancy.

Divination by means of the ascent or motion of smoke.

Ceromancy.

Divination by dropping melted wax in water.

Chartomancy.

Divination by written paper or by cards.

Cleromancy.

A divination by throwing dice or casting lots.

Coscinomancy.

Divination by means of a suspended sieve.

Crystallomancy.

Divination by means of a crystal or other transparent body, especially a beryl.

Dactyliomancy.
Divination by means of finger rings.

Daphnomancy.
Divination by means of a laurel.

Demonomagy.
Magic in which the name of demons is invoked; black or infernal magic.

Enoptomancy.
Divination by the use of a mirror.

Gastromancy.
1. A kind of divination by means of words seemingly uttered from the stomach.
2. A species of divination by means of glasses or other round, transparent vessels, in the center of which figures are supposed to appear by magic art.

Geomancy.
A kind of divination by means of figures or lines, formed by little dots or points, originally on the earth, and latterly on paper.

Gyromancy.
A kind of divination performed by drawing a ring or circle and walking in or around it.

Hieromancy.

Divination by observing the objects offered in sacrifice.

Hydromancy.

Divination by means of water; practiced by the ancients.

Ichthyomancy.

Divination by the heads or the entrails of fishes.

Lecanomancy.

Divination practiced with water in a basin, by throwing three stones into it, and invoking the demon whose aid was sought.

Lithomancy.

The art of divination by means of stones.

Metopomancy.

The practice of fortune telling by physiognomy.

Nomancy.

The art or practice of divining the destiny of persons by the letters which form their names.

Necromancy.

The art of revealing future events by means of a pretended communication with the dead; the *black art;* hence, magic in general.

Omphalomancy.
Divination by means of a child's navel, to learn how many children the mother may have.

Oneiromancy.
Divination by means of dreams.

Onomancy.
Divination by the letters of a name; Nomancy.

Onychomancy.
Divination by the nails.

Ophiomancy.
Divination by serpents, as by their manner of eating, or by their coils.

Ornithomancy.
Divination by means of birds, their flight, etc.

Osteomanty.
Divination by means of bones.

Pedomancy.
Divination by examining the soles of the feet.

Pyromancy.
Fire, divination by fire.

Psychomancy.
Divination by consulting the souls of the dead.

Rhapsodomancy.

Divination by means of verses.

Rhabdomancy.

Divination by rods.

Stichomancy.

Divination by lines or passages of books, taken at hazard.

Stigonomancy.

Divination by writing on the bark of a tree.

Sciomancy.

Divination by means of shadows.

INDEX.

ISMS.

DOCTRINAL AND SECTARIAN ISMS.

Ag-nos'ti-cism 13	Cer'e-mo'ni-al-ism 20
Ar-min'i-an 14	Cor-po're-al-ism . . 20
Au'to-the-ism . . 14	Cos'mo-the'ism . . 20
An'ti-no'mi-an-ism . . 14	Chil'i-asm 21
A-pos'ta-sy 15	Cal'vin-ism 21
As-cet'i-cism 15	
Al'lo-the-ism 15	Dru'id-ism 21
An'a-bap'tism 15	Dru'id 22
An'gli-can-ism 16	De-mo'ni-an-ism . . 22
An'thro-pop'a-thism . 16	De'mon-ol'a-try 22
Au'gus-tin'i an-ism . 16	Dog'ma-tism 22
A'ri-an-ism . . . 16	Du'al-ism 22
A-nath'e-ma-tism . 16	Di'the-ism 22
	De'ism 22
Bab'ism . . . 17	Dol'lard-ism 23
Ben'tham-ism . . 17	Dollard . . . 23
Ba'al-ism 17	Don'a-tism 23
Brah'man-ism 18	Don'a-tist . . 23
Boodh 18	De'mon-ism 23
Boodh'ism 18	De-nom'i-na'tion-al-ism 23
Bud'dhism . . . 18	
Bi'the-ism 19	Eu-no'mi-an 23
	Eth'ni-cism 24
Con'sub-stan'tial-ism . 19	Eu-hem'er-ism 24
Con'gre-ga'tion-al-ism 19	E-van'gel-ism 24
Cler'ic-al-ism . . . 20	Ex'or-cism . . . 24
Cen'o-bi-tism 20	Es'se-nism . . . 24

150

Eu-tych'i-an-ism	24
Es-tab'lish-men-ta'ri-an	25
E-ras'tian-ism	25
Es'o-ter'ic-ism	25
Fe'tich-ism	26
Form'al-ism	26
Fam'i-lism	26
Fa-nat'i-cism	26
Fa'tal-ism	27
Gal'li-can-ism	27
Ge-ne'van-ism	27
Gnos'ti-cism	27
Hen'o-the-ism	27
Hi'er-arch'ism	28
Hu-man'i-ta'ri-an-ism	28
Hy'lism	28
Hy-lop'a-thism	28
Hy'lo-the-ism	29
I-de'al-ism	29
Im'ma-te'ri-al-ism	29
I-den'tism	29
Im-pe'ri-al-ism	30
In'fra-lap-sa'ri-an-ism	30
Jes'u-it-ism	30
Jan'sen-ism	31
Ka'ra-ism	31
Lu'ther-an-ism	31
Lat'i-tu'di-na'ri-an-ism	31
Lab'a-dist	32
La'ma-ism	32
Ma'gi-an-ism	32
Man'i-che-ism	32
Ma-te'ri-al-ism	32
Me-temp'sy-cho'sis	33
Mo-ham'med-an-ism	33
Mo-nas'ti-cism	33
Mo-noth'e-lite	33
Mon'o-the-ism	33
Mon'ta-nist	33
Mys'ti-cism	34
Mil-len'ni-an-ism	34
Mis'o-the'ism	35
Mo'dal-ist	35
Mo'lin-ism	35
Mon'o-psy'chism	35
Mac'e-do'ni-an-ism	35
Male-branch'ism	35
Man'i-che-ism	36
Na'tiv-ism	36
Nat'u-ral-ism	36
Ni'cene	36
No-va'tian-ism	37
Naz'a-ri-tism	37
Ne'o-no'mi-an-ism	37
Ne'o-pla'to-nism	37
Or'i-gen-ism	38
Ob-scur'an-tism	38
Op'ti-mism	38
Oc-ca'sion-al-ism	38
Oc-cult'ism	39
Par'tial-ism	39
Pa'gan-ism	39
Prop'a-gan'dism	39
Pre-mon'stra-ten'sian	39
Pres'by-te'ri-an-ism	40
Plym'outh Breth'ren	40
Pol'y-the-ism	40
Pos'i-tiv-ism	40

152   INDEX.

Prel'a-tism 41
Pa'tri-arch-ism 41
Pa'tri-pas'sian 41
Pau'li-cian 41
Per-fec'tion-ism 41
Pan'the-ism 41
Pla'ton-ism . . . 42
Plo'ti-nist 42
Pha-lan'ster-ism 42
Phar'i-sa-ism 42
Pi'e-tism . . . 43
Psy'chism 43
Pil'lar-ist . 43
Pa'tri-pas'sians . . 44
Pe'do-bap'tism . . . 44
Psy'cho-pan'ny-chism . . 44
Pur'ga-to-ry 44
Pur'i-tan-ism 44
Pu'sey-ism 44
Prot'est-ant'ism 45
Psi-lan'thro-pism 45
Pre-des'ti-na'ri-an-ism . 45
Prel'a-tist 45
Pyr'rho-nism 45
Py-thag'o-rism 46

Qui'et-ism 46

Ra'tion-al-ism 46
Ro'man-ism 46
Re-cu'sant 47

Sab'ba-tism . . . 47
Sa'tan-ism 47
Shin'to-ism 47
Scho-las'ti-cism . 47
Sha'min-ism 48

Sec-ta'ri-an-ism 48
Su'pra-lap-sa'ri-ans 49
Sto'i-cism 49
Su'fism 50
Swe'den-bor'gi-an-ism . 50
Su'per-nat'u-ral-ism . 50
Syn'cre-tism 51
Spi'no-zism 51
Spir'it-u-al-ism 51
Sab'ba-ta'ri-an-ism . . . 51
Sa-bel'li-an-ism 52
Sa'bi-an-ism 52
Sen'ti-ment 52
Sen'ti-ment'al 54
Sac'ra-ment'al-ism . 54
Sac'ra-men-ta'ri-an 55
So-cin'i-an-ism . . 55
Skep'ti-cism . 55
Sen'ti-ment'al-ism 56
Schwenk'feld-i-an . . 56

Tran'scen-den'tal-ism . 56
Tran'scen-den'tal . . 56
Tav'ism 58
The-oc'ra-sy 58
The-od'i-cy 58
Tri'the-ism 58
The-os'o-phy 59
The-og'o-nism 60
The'ism . . . 61
The-os'o-phism . 61

Ul'tra-mon'ta-nism . . 61
U'ni-ta'ri-an-ism . . 61
U'ni-ver'sal-ism . 61
U-til'i-ta'ri-an-ism 62

INDEX.

CIVIC ISMS.

An'arch-ism	63	Le-git'i-mism	70
An'ti-civ'ism	63	Lib'er-al-ism	71
Boy'cott-ism	63	Mach'i-a-vel'ian-ism	71
Bu-reau'cra-cy	63	Mil'i-tar-ism	71
Bi-met'al-lism	64	Mal-thu'sian-ism	71
Col-lect'iv-ism	64	Nep'o-tism	71
Chart'ism	64	Ni'hil-ism	71
Civ'ism	64	Na'tion-al-ism	72
Cæ'sar-ism	64		
Cyph'o-nism	65		
Com'mu-nal-ism	65	Ol'i-gar'chy	72
Com'mu-nism	65	Op'ti-ma-cy	72
Car'bo-na'rism	65		
Cen'tral-ism	66	Pa'tri-ot-ism	73
Con-serv'a-tism	66	Phal'an-ste'ri-an-ism	73
Con'sti-tu'tion-al-ism	66	Pan-hel'len-ism	73
Con-ven'tion-al-ism	66	Pan-is'lam-ism	73
Con'vict-ism	67	Pan'sla'vism	73
		Pa-ter'nal-ism	73
Doc'tri-na'ri-an-ism	67	Pro-tec'tion-ism	74
De-moc'ra-tism	67		
Des'po-tism	68	Rad'i-cal-ism	74
Dem'a-gog-ism	68	Roy'al-ism	74
		Re-pub'li-can-ism	74
Ex-clu'sion-ism	68		
		Sec'tion-al-ism	75
Fe'ni-an-ism	68	So'cial-ism	75
Feu'dal-ism	68	Saint'-Si-mo'ni-an-ism	75
Fil'i-bus'ter-ism	69		
		To'ry-ism	76
In-civ'ism	69	The-oc'racy	76
In'di-vid'u-al-ism	69		
		Van'dal-ism	76
Jac'o-bin-ism	69	Vol'un-ta-ry-ism	77
		Voo'doo-ism	77
Know'noth'ing-ism	70		

OLOGIES.

THEORETICAL AND SCIENTIFIC.

Ae'ti-ol'o-gy	78	Hi'er-ol'o-gy	83
Ag'noi-ol'o-gy	78	Ho-rol'o-gy	83
Ag'ri-ol'o-gy	78	Hy-drol'o-gy	83
A-le'thi-ol'o-gy	78		
Am'phi-bol'o-gy	78	Ich'thy-ol'o-gy	83
An'gel-ol'o-gy	79	I'co-nol'o-gy	84
An'thro-pol'o-gy	79		
An'e-mol'o-gy	79	Me'te-or-ol'o-gy	84
An'ge-ol'o-gy	79	Min'er-al'o-gy	84
An'thro-pop'a-thy	79	My-ol'o-gy	84
Ar'che-ol'o-gy	80	My-thol'o-gy	84
As-trol'o-gy	80		
Au'gur	80	Ne-crol'o-gy	84
As'tro-the-ol'o-gy	84	Ne-ol'o-gy	84
As'the-nol'o-gy	81	Neu-rol'o-gy	85
		No-sol'o-gy	85
Bat-tol'o-gy	81	Nu-mis'ma-tol'o-gy	85
Bi-ol'o-gy	81		
		On-tol'o-gy	85
Ce-tol'o-gy	81	O'phi-ol'o-gy	85
Chi-rol'o-gy	81	Or'ni-thol'o-gy	85
Chi'ro-man'cy	81	O-rol'o-gy	85
Chro-nol'o-gy	81	Or-thol'o-gy	85
Con-chol'o-gy	82	Os'te-ol'o-gy	86
Cos-mol'o-gy	82		
Cra'ni-ol'o-gy	82	Pa'le-ol'o-gy	86
		Pa'le-on-tol'o-gy	86
Dem'o-nol'o-gy	82	Pan-tol'o-gy	86
		Phre-nol'o-gy	86
Ec-cle'si-ol'o-gy	82	Phi-lol'o-gy	86
Es-thet'i-cism	82	Phy-tol'o-gy	87
Eu-chol'o-gy	83	Phys'i-ol'o-gy	87
Eth-nol'o-gy	83	Phys'i-co-the-ol'o-gy	87
		Pneu'ma-tol'o-gy	87
Ge-ol'o-gy	83	Psy-chol'o-gy	87
Gi'gau-tol'o-gy	83	Pseu-dol'o-gy	87

INDEX. 155

Py-rol'o-gy	87	So'ma-tol'o-gy	89
Pyr'e-tol'o-gy	88		
Pa-thog'no-my	88		
Phar'ma-col'o-gy	88	Ter'mi-nol'o-gy	89
Pho-tol'o-gy	88	Tox'i-col'o-gy	89
Pho-nol'o-gy	88	Tro-pol'o-gy	89
Pab-dol'o-gy	88		
Pa-thol'o-gy	88		
Pan'the-ol'o-gy	88	U'ra-nol'o-gy	89

MISCELLANY.

Ar'yan	93	An'i-mal-ism	98
Art	93	An'i-mal'cu-lism	99
A-nal'o-gy	94	At'om-ism	99
A-nal'o-gism	95	A-ver'ro-ism	99
A-nat'o-mism	95		
An'thro-pos'co-py	95	Bac'cha-na'li-an-ism	100
Al'ien-ism	95	Bar'ba-rism	100
An-thro-pol'a-try	95	Burk'ism	100
As-trol'a-try	95	Bap'tist	100
At'a-vism	96		
An-drog'y-nism	96	Cyn'i-cism	101
An'glo-Sax'on-ism	96	Car'di-nal Vir'tues	101
An'ti-Christ	96	Cer'tain-ties	101
A-pol'o-get'ics	96	Cas'u-ist-ry	101
Af'ri-can-ism	96	Chris'tian Sci'ence	102
Al'tru-ism	96	Char'la-tan-ism	102
An-tich'ro-nism	97	Cli'quism	102
Ag'o-nism	97	Con-cep'tu-al-ism	103
Ath'a-na'sian	97	Crit'i-cism	103
A'the-ism	97	Cru-sade'	103
A-gra'ri-an-ism	97		
Al'co-hol-ism	97	Death	103
An-ach'ro-nism	98	Doc'trine	104
Ab'sen-tee'ism	98	Dog'ma	105
Ab'sin-thism	98	De'mon-ol'a-try	106
Ab'so-lu'tism	98	Dar'win-ism	106
Ac'ro-bat-ism	98	Dil'et-tan'te-ism	107

INDEX.

Ev′o-lu′tion The′o-ry	107
Em-pir′i-cism	110
Ec-lec′ti-cism	110
E′go-ism	110
E′le-at′i-cism	111
Ex-ter′nal-ism	111
Ex-pe′ri-en′tial-ism	111
Ep′i-cu-re′an-ism	111
Eu-de′mon-ism	111
Eu-hem′er-ism	112
E-the′re-al-ism	112
Fate of the Apostles	112
Faith	114
Fa′bi-an	114
Gyn′e-ol′a-try	114
He′lot	115
Ha′gi-ol′a-try	115
He′li-ol′a-try	115
Hu′man-ism	115
I-con′o-clasm	115
I-con′o-clast	116
I′co-nol′a-try	116
Ig′nis fat′u-us	116
Ju′da-ism	116
Life	117
Leg′end	117
Meth′od	118
Mag′ic	119
Mon′ism	119
Ma′ri-ol′a-try	120
Mo-ra′vi-an-ism	120
Mes′mer-ism	120

Mount′e-bank	120
Mem′non	120
Me-men′to mo′ri	120
Mem′o-ra-bil′i-a	121
Mir′a-cle	121
Mi-rage′	121
Nom′i-nal-ism	122
Nick	122
Ne-crol′a-try	122
Op′ti-mism	122
Os′tra-cism	122
Pyth′i-an	122
Pyth′o-ness	122
Phys′i-ol′a-try	123
Pau′per-ism	123
Pet′al-ism	123
Pes′si-mism	123
Par′see-ism	123
Par′a-si′tism	123
Phar′i-sa-ism	123
Phe-nom′e-non	124
Psy′chi-cal	124
Par′the-non	125
Pros′e-ly-tism	125
Pro-vin′cial-ism	125
Pur′ism	125
Pu′tan-ism	125
Pan-the′on	125
Pan′de-mo′ni-um	125
Pyth′o-nism	125
Quid′nunc	126
Quix′ot-ism	126
Rhap′so-dy	126
Rab′bi	126

Rab'bin-ism 126	The-ol'o-gy 134
Re'al-ism 126	The Mind Cure 136
Re-lig'ion 127	The Bible 139
Ros'i-cru'cians 127	The'o-ry 139
	The'ur-gy 140
Sci'ence 127	Trib'al-ism 140
Syl'lo-gism 129	The'mis 140
Syn'cre-tism 129	Tan'ta-lism 141
Sys'tem 129	Tal'mud 141
Sav'a-gism 129	Tru'ism 141
Scamp'ism 129	
Scho-las'ti-cism 129	Ul'tra-ism 141
Scoun'drel-ism . . . 129	U-to'pi-a 141
Sen-sa'tion-al-ism 130	
Sci'o-lism 130	Ver-nac'u-lar-ism 141
Sen'su-al-ism 130	Ven-tril'o-quism 142
Schism 130	Vul'gar-ism 142
So'ma-tist 130	
Sto'ic-al 131	Wor'ship 142
Su'per-sti'tion . . . 131	Wit'ti-cism 142
	Whig'ism 142
The Seven Bibles of the	
World 132	Zy-mol'o-gy 142
Tra-di'tion-al-ism . . 133	Zo-ol'o-gy 142

DIVINATION.

An'thra-co-man'cy 143	Bel'o-man'cy . . . 145
An'thro-po-man'cy . . . 143	Bib'li-o-man'cy 145
A-rus'pi-cy 143	
As-trag'al-o-man'cy . . 144	
Aus'tro-man'cy . . . 144	Cap'no-man'cy 145
Ax-in'o-man'cy . . 144	Cer'o-man'cy 145
A-lec'try-o-man'cy . . 144	Char'to-man'cy 145
A-leu'ro-man'cy . . 144	Cler'o-man'cy 145
Al'o-man'cy . 144	Cos-cin'o-man'cy . . 145
Al-phit'o-man'cy . . 144	Crys'tal-lo-man'cy 145
A'er-o-man'cy . . . 144	

INDEX.

Dac-tyl'i-o-man'cy 146
Daph'no-man'cy . . . 146
De'mon-om'a-gy 146

En-op'to-man'cy 146

Gas'tro-man'cy 146
Ge'o-man'cy 146
Gyr'o-man'cy 146

Hi'er-o-man'cy 147
Hy'dro-man'cy 147

Ich'thy-o-man'cy 147

Le-can'o-man'cy 147
Lith'o-man'cy 147

Met'o-po-man'cy 147

No'man-cy 147
Nec'ro-man'cy 147

Om'pha-lo-man'cy 148
O-nei'ro-man'cy 148
On'o-man'cy 148
On'y-cho-man'cy . . . 148
O'phi-o-man'cy 148
Or-nith'o-man'cy 148
Os'te-o-man'ty 148

Ped'o-man'cy 148
Pyr'o-man'cy 148
Psy'cho-man'cy 148

Rhap'so-do-man'cy 149
Rhab'do-man'cy 149

Stich'o-man'cy 149
Stig'o-no-man'cy 149
Sci'o-man'cy 149

www.ingramcontent.com/pod-product-compliance
Lightning Source LLC
Chambersburg PA
CBHW030257170426
43202CB00009B/782